You Belong

Letters, Love, and Lessons from Women
Who Reclaimed Their Wholeness

HANNA OLIVAS

Along With 16 Inspiring Authors

ISBN: 978-1-969463-86-0

TABLE OF CONTENTS

INTRODUCTION

You've found your way to these pages for a reason.

Maybe you've felt out of place in your own life. Maybe you've been carrying questions that don't have easy answers. Or maybe you've simply needed a quiet space to land—a space where you're not expected to perform, fix, or explain. Just be.

You Belong was born from that ache. The silent, sacred question so many women carry: *Do I really belong?*

Here. In this body. In this season. In this version of myself.

Inside this book, you'll find letters—soft, strong, and searching. Written by women who have lived through grief, transitions, self-doubt, and unexpected detours. Women who've done the slow, tender work of coming home to themselves. These are not loud declarations or polished success stories. They're real. Honest. Often unfinished.

Each chapter offers a moment of reflection, a breath of reassurance, a flicker of light in the dark. These letters are not written *to* you, but you'll find yourself in them—because they're written *for* the woman who's learning to trust herself again.

If you're in a season of uncertainty, if you've lost sight of your worth, or if you just need to hear something kind for once—let this book be a companion.

You don't have to have all the answers. You don't have to be anywhere other than where you are.

You belong.
Right here. Right now. Just as you are.

Hanna Olivas

Founder and CEO of SHE RISES STUDIOS

https://www.linkedin.com/company/she-rises-studios/
https://www.facebook.com/sherisesstudios
https://www.instagram.com/sherisesstudios_llc/
www.SheRisesStudios.com

Author, Speaker, and Founder. Hanna was born and raised in Las Vegas, Nevada, and has paved her way to becoming one of the most influential women of 2022. Hanna is the co-founder of She Rises Studios and the founder of the Brave & Beautiful Blood Cancer Foundation. Her journey started in 2017 when she was first diagnosed with Multiple Myeloma, an incurable blood cancer. Now more than ever, her focus is to empower other women to become leaders because The Future is Female. She is currently traveling and speaking publicly to women to educate them on entrepreneurship, leadership, and owning the female power within.

You Belong

By Hanna Olivas

Belonging is one of those words we hear all the time, yet somehow spend half our lives chasing. It sounds simple, but if you're a woman, especially a woman with dreams, ambition, culture, resilience, and a story, you know belonging isn't simple at all. For many of us, it's a journey paved with silence, survival, loss, reinvention, and finally, that moment when you decide: I belong because I say so.

I didn't grow up understanding belonging. My childhood was loving but complicated. I was raised by a single mother and grandparents who gave everything they had to keep our world stitched together. We didn't have much, but we had heart. We had grit. We had faith. We had a loud, colorful, imperfect family that taught me early what love looked like and what struggle felt like.

Still, I never quite felt like I fit anywhere. I was too Latina for some rooms, not Latina enough for others. Too outspoken in some circles, too emotional in others. Too ambitious for people who thought girls like me should stay quiet. Too soft-hearted for people who thought strength meant coldness. Too much for those who preferred convenience. Not enough for those who wanted perfection.

That's the thing about belonging.

We often spend our earliest years trying to become someone who will be accepted, not realizing we're molding ourselves into a shape that was never ours.

As a girl, I learned to adapt. Like many young women, I learned to read the room before I ever learned to read my own emotions. I learned to shrink myself in places that demanded silence. I learned to overachieve in places that valued performance over authenticity. I learned to be tough, even when I was breaking.

And like countless women, I learned these lessons quietly.

The world doesn't teach girls to belong to themselves. It teaches us to belong to expectations.

But life has a way of unteaching us the lies we swallow.

For me, belonging wasn't a single moment. It wasn't a lightning strike. It was a series of heartbreaks, losses, awakenings, and hard-won victories that forced me to confront one simple truth:

I had been looking for belonging in everyone but myself.

Loss has a way of clearing out illusions. When I lost my son Mario, it changed something in me forever. I won't go into the details, because the pain is still too real, too sacred, too heavy. But I will say this: that loss broke me open. It made me question everything, who I was, why I was here, how I could possibly go on.

And yet, something inside me survived.

That's when belonging whispered its first real truth.

"You belong to your own strength, even when you feel shattered."

From the outside, women often look like we have it all under control. We hold families together. We work two or three jobs. We build businesses. We show up for everyone else, even when we're running on empty. We forgive more than we should. We push through pain we never talk about. We reinvent ourselves in silence. We rise in the dark long before anyone sees the light.

But belonging doesn't come from performing strength.

It comes from honoring our humanity.

My early adulthood brought more lessons like this, hard ones. I faced trauma, fear, and heartbreak no woman deserves. Abuse taught me about survival. Betrayal taught me about boundaries. Illness taught me about fragility. Cancer taught me about courage I didn't know I had. Nearly losing myself taught me that belonging isn't found in people, it's found in purpose.

And still, even then, I was searching.

I thought belonging would show up when I built my business. When I became successful. When I stepped onto stages. When I helped thousands of women rise. When I checked the boxes of achievement. When I proved myself to the world.

But here's the truth I finally learned.

Belonging does not come from accomplishment. It comes from alignment.

Women in business know this better than anyone.

We walk into boardrooms where we are underestimated before we even speak.

We pitch ideas that get dismissed until a man repeats them.

We build companies while raising families, fighting self-doubt, and navigating trauma.

We sit at tables where we are tolerated, not celebrated.

We hustle twice as hard for half the credit.

We endure whispers, competition, jealousy, and sabotage.

We bend so much for people who will never bend for us.

And yet, we rise anyway.

Not because we are superhuman, but because we've learned to create belonging in places that were never designed for us.

The first time I walked into a room full of powerful entrepreneurs, I felt like an impostor. I wasn't born into wealth. I didn't come from a family of connections. I didn't speak the language of boardrooms. I didn't have investors behind me. I was a Latina mother with big dreams, a bigger heart, and a fire that refused to die.

But the moment I decided that my story, my scars, and my strength were not weaknesses, but power that's when everything began to change.

I stopped trying to belong to the room.

I made the room belong to me.

That shift didn't happen overnight. It came after years of being overlooked. After mistreatment. After countless times when I was underestimated. After navigating a business world that didn't create space for women who speak truth, lead from the heart, and challenge broken systems.

Especially when those systems benefit from us staying silent.

Belonging in business is different for women. We bring our entire selves, our families, our culture, our resilience, our intuition, our trauma, and our magic. We don't get to separate our personal and professional lives the way men do. We carry everything with us, and we still excel.

Women entrepreneurs are warriors wrapped in grace.

Young women especially need to hear this. You don't need to change who you are to belong. You don't need to lose yourself to fit into rooms that don't honor you. Where you belong will feel like oxygen, not suffocation. The right people won't ask you to shrink. The right opportunities won't require you to betray yourself. The right path will make you feel more like you, not less.

As I built She Rises Studios, FENIX, our global women's networks, our publishing houses, magazines, award shows, and events, I saw firsthand what happens when women finally realize they belong.

They stop apologizing.

They start leading.

They speak louder.

They stand taller.

They take risks.

They break barriers.

They help other women rise.

They stop chasing validation and start building legacy.

The beautiful thing about belonging is this,

When one woman claims her place, she creates space for hundreds more.

That's why I share my story. Not because it's easy, but because someone out there needs to know she isn't the only one who has struggled to find where she fits. Someone needs to know that healing is possible. Someone needs to know that her story matters. Someone needs to know that her dreams aren't too big. Someone needs to know that she isn't broken, she's becoming.

Belonging isn't about perfection. It's about permission.

Permission to be real.

Permission to evolve.

Permission to walk away from places that don't honor you.

Permission to rewrite your story.

Permission to feel everything.

Permission to create your own community.

Permission to take up space without apologizing.

Permission to say, "I belong here," even before anyone understands why.

One of the biggest lessons I've learned is this,

You don't need people to agree with your purpose for it to be your purpose.

Not everyone will understand you.

Not everyone will support you.

Not everyone will like you.

Not everyone will root for you.

And that's okay.

You don't belong to their expectations.

You belong to your calling.

And your calling will sometimes take you into places where you stand alone before you stand with others.

There have been seasons in my life where I felt misunderstood, judged, even attacked. There were times when people I loved turned against me. Times when I disappointed others and had to face my own mistakes. Times when my reputation was on the line. Times when I questioned whether I deserved to be in leadership at all.

But here's the thing about belonging,

It doesn't disappear just because life gets messy.

Belonging deepens through honesty.

I've made mistakes.

I've trusted the wrong people.

I've given more than I received.

I've lost myself in the process of helping others.

I've been hurt, betrayed, criticized, and misunderstood.

I've had to rebuild my business, my health, my peace, and my identity more times than I care to count.

And yet, here I stand.

Still rising.

Still healing.

Still learning.

Still leading.

Still belonging.

Not because life has been easy, but because purpose has been louder than pain.

Every woman I've met, young or old, a student or CEO, a mother, survivor, creator, entrepreneur, has navigated her own battle with belonging. And almost all of them have one thing in common,

They spent years believing they were alone.

They weren't.

You aren't either.

Belonging is not something you wait to be invited into.

It's something you step into boldly, even when your voice shakes.

It's choosing yourself in a world that constantly tells you to choose everything else first.

It's honoring your story instead of hiding it.

It's believing that your voice matters, even when you've been silenced before.

It's refusing to shrink for people who refuse to grow.

It's recognizing that your differences are your destiny.

It's knowing that every version of you, hurt, healed, lost, rising, broken, blooming deserves space.

Belonging is not about being perfect.

Belonging is about being whole.

You belong in every chapter of your life, even the ones that broke you.

You belong in every dream, even the ones that scare you.

You belong in every room where your purpose leads you.

You belong in conversations where your ideas shift atmospheres.

You belong in leadership, even if you're the first in your family to get there.

You belong in healing, even if you've been hurt deeply.

You belong in joy, even if you've lived through years of sorrow.

You belong in abundance, even if you were taught to settle.

You belong in success, even if people said you never would rise.

You belong in love, even if your heart has been broken.

You belong in power, even if you were taught to play small.

And above all, you belong in your own life.

The one you desire. The one you imagine. The one you're building brick by brick, choice by choice, day by day.

Belonging begins the moment you decide your worth is not negotiable.

It starts when you realize,

You do not have to earn belonging. You already are it.

And that is what I want every woman to know.

You belong.

In your story.

In your strength.

In your softness.

In your ambition.

In your culture.

In your voice.

In your truth.

In your healing.

In the rooms you create.

In the rooms you transform.

In the rooms that once made you question yourself.

In the world you are shaping simply by being who you are.

You belong not because someone chose you,

but because you finally chose yourself.

And that, my love, is where the real journey begins.

XOXO,
Hanna

Nakeida Edmundson

Founder of G.R.O.W.T.H Getting Rid of Worry, Trouble & Hurt

Hello, My name is Nakeida. I was born and raised in Paterson, New Jersey. I moved to Georgia in my early 20's for a fresh start. I am a divorced mother of two awesome children who I adore and love deeply. I am the Founder of G.R.O.W.T.H - Getting Rid of Worry, Trouble & Hurt. I started this organization after going through a very difficult divorce. I wanted to help women who were facing hardships and challenging times, such as, domestic violence and/or homelessness. Helping other women get back on their feet and regain their confidence and worth is a passion of mine. I remember a time when I needed help and reassurance that I mattered and that I could overcome obstacles. As women we have to remember that we are strong and resilient.

Dear Beautiful You

By Nakeida Edmundson

Dear Beautiful You,

I hope this letter finds you in a moment of calmness, a breath between the chaos, and a pause in the rush. Because I want you to hear this clearly: **You are enough. You are beautiful. You are worthy!**

Girl! You are amazing! Not because of the way you look, the titles you hold, or the roles you play. But because you exist. Because you feel deeply. Because you carry love, strength, and resilience in your bones.

I see you. Not just the surface you show the world but the real you. The one who's faced storms, hidden tears, and kept going anyway. The one who wakes up every day carrying hopes, worries, dreams, and fears all at once.

You've been taught to chase perfection, to shrink your light, and even to apologize for taking up space. But I'm here to remind you: You don't need fixing. You don't need permission. You don't need to be more of anything to be loved.

I can now say these things to you and to myself boldly and with confidence.

I remember a time when I was so confident. I knew my worth; I knew I was beautiful, inside and out. I had a lot to offer, and my presence was known, respected, and appreciated.

It's amazing how quickly my self-esteem was taken away. How I went from being so confident and happy in the skin I was in to not wanting to leave the house.

I allowed myself to be validated by a man who worked hard to break me. It's nothing like having all this confidence and being happy with myself only to be chopped down so bad that I lost myself. I forgot who I was. I forgot my worth. Until one day, I was tired of feeling worthless and I knew I had to gain my confidence back if I wanted to continue living my life to the fullest. I wanted to be an example to my daughter. How could I teach her that it is important to know her worth and to not settle if I was feeling less than a woman? One day, it was like someone whispered to me on the hardest days: **You are enough, exactly as you are.**

No matter what that man or anyone else told me, I realized that there was no need for me to change, to fix, or to prove myself to anyone. My worth wasn't in what I did or how I looked. It was simply me being me. The unique soul that I am, with my laughter, my scars, my fierce heart, and gentle spirit.

My beautiful friend, I want you to know your scars tell stories of survival. Your laughter is a rebellion against pain. Your softness is not weakness; it's power. And your presence, just as it is, makes this world better.

So, wear your truth boldly. Speak with passion and tenderness. Let your joy be loud. Let your tears be sacred.

When you feel invisible, when doubts creep in like shadows, remember that your presence lights up spaces others don't even realize are dark. When they tried to bury you, they didn't know you were a seed and would sprout up into a more beautiful vision. You are a force not because you try to be, but because you simply are, and it comes naturally to you.

There's beauty in your softness, strength in your kindness, and magic in your imperfections. You don't have to earn love or respect; you deserve it just for showing up and being the amazing person you are.

So today, when you look in the mirror, do it with kindness. Speak to yourself with love and inspiration like you would to your best friend.

Because, truly, you are a treasure, a whole, radiant, and powerful treasure.

And if ever you forget or if the world tries to tell you otherwise, this letter is your reminder:

You are more than enough. You are beautiful beyond measure, and friend, I love that for you.

With all my heart,
Nakeida
Someone who believes in you

Holly Cotton

HC Media
Wellness Expert, Author, Media Personality

https://www.linkedin.com/in/holly-cotton-3342a6227/
www.instagram.com/hollycotton_
www.hollycotton.com
www.yourmindyourmagic.com

Holly Cotton blends her expertise as a nurse and renowned Wellness Expert with self-care and mental health advocacy. She is a Media Personality, Author, women's health and mental health advocate. She inspires and guides others to transform their lives through her book collection of books. Holly holds a Master's Degree in Nursing and has leveraged her medical expertise to advance her nursing career and establish herself as a distinguished authority in health and wellness, being voted as one of the "Top 150 Nurses" by the Houston Chronicle. She is the founder of, Your Mind, Your Magic, a global youth initiative providing affirmation books and free mental wellness resources for kids.

Claiming Space Without an Apology

By Holly Cotton

There's something no one tells you when your life shatters. Even when people show up, you can still feel completely alone. When I was diagnosed with breast cancer, I was young, healthy, and had a whole planned-out life ahead of me. I was a mom, a nurse, and a woman who knew how to keep it all together. And suddenly, I was a patient. A statistic. A question mark in my own future. Everyone had something kind to say. "You're strong." "You've got this." "You'll beat it." They meant well, but none of it touched the storm I was carrying inside.

What they didn't see was the silent grief, the fear that crept in between appointments, the loss of control over my own body, and the isolation that wrapped around me like a second skin. I didn't feel strong. I didn't feel like I was "handling it." I felt cracked open in a way no one around me could truly understand. And that's when it hit me: I was surrounded by people, but I had never felt more disconnected. Not because they didn't care, but because they didn't get it. They didn't know what it felt like to plan a future and then suddenly question if you'd even have one. They didn't know the kind of mourning that happens when you lose a version of yourself that didn't get a chance to fully live. It wasn't that I didn't belong to them; I just didn't belong to myself anymore. And that was the most painful part of it all, the way trauma quietly separates you from the person you used to be, and no one tells you how to find your way back. But that disconnection? That silence? That loneliness? It became the beginning of something I didn't expect.

I didn't recognize myself anymore. Not just in the mirror, but in the silence after everyone left. In the in-between spaces. In the new version of me that no one knew how to hold. The woman I was before cancer didn't make it to the other side. She was gone. And what I was left with was... new me. Raw. Unfiltered. Tired of pretending I was okay just so other people wouldn't feel uncomfortable. And so, I started writing, honestly. Not for a blog. Not for a book. Just for me to figure out what this new belonging even looked like. Who was I after cancer? Where did I fit in when my world had split wide open, but everyone else's kept moving like nothing happened? The truth is, I felt jealous sometimes. Resentful even.

People around me were planning vacations, brunching on weekends, scrolling, and laughing about simple things. Meanwhile, I was counting down the days to my next surgery, researching what foods wouldn't make me sick, and wondering if I'd live long enough to see my son graduate. And then I'd feel guilty for those feelings. For the resentment of watching others live effortlessly. I felt guilty for not being grateful just to be alive.

But here's what no one says: It's okay to be grateful and grieving at the same time. It's okay to feel like you're drowning in a sea of people who are just casually wading through their day. It took me time to forgive the world for not breaking with me. And even more time to forgive myself for changing. I had to learn that belonging wasn't about people understanding what I was going through. It wasn't about fitting back into the same spaces. It was about showing up as this new version of me, scars, softness, fire, and all.

I wrote this down one day in my journal: "Maybe I don't need to go back to who I was." So I stopped trying to be who I was before. I stopped forcing connections that couldn't hold me anymore. And I started being honest, with myself first. That I was lonely. That I was afraid. That I didn't want to have to be strong every day. That I wanted to feel seen, really seen, and not just praised for being resilient. I started softening into who I was now. Letting myself belong to this new body. This new season. Letting my voice tremble if it needed to. Letting my truth exist even if it makes other people uncomfortable. And that's when I began to find it. That quiet, sacred place inside me that whispered, "You're still here. And that's more than enough." There's something deeply humbling about not being able to lift your arms to put your hair in a ponytail. It sounds small. But when you've spent your life being strong physically, emotionally, and spiritually, it shakes something in you.

I remember standing in the mirror after surgery, my arms barely moving, looking at a body I didn't recognize anymore. Scars. The body that used to run, press weights, and flex confidently in the mirror was now stitched, swollen, and still. I couldn't work out like I used to. I couldn't even pick up a dumbbell. I had to redefine what "strong" meant, not just in my body, but in my identity. And that part hurt more than the healing wounds. So much of who I believed I was resilient, fit, unstoppable, was tied to how I moved through the world. Suddenly, that movement was slower, more fragile, more deliberate. I had to meet myself again in pieces. In tiny wins. In new goals that didn't involve sweat but softness. The first time I raised my arms above my head without pain, I cried. Not because of the movement, but because it reminded me I was still here. Still becoming.

That's when I started to shift. Not back into the woman I was before, but into the woman I was becoming, one stretch, one journal page, one breath at a time. And for the first time since my diagnosis, I asked a different question. Not "Why me?" But "Why not me?" Why not be the one who comes back stronger, not just in muscles, but in purpose? Why not be the one who redefines what it means to belong in her body again, even after it's changed? Why not take the pieces I thought I lost and use them to build something I'd never imagined? That question unlocked something in me. It stopped being about survival. It became about intention. If I had to fight to be here, then I was going to be here. Fully. Loudly. Unapologetically. That was the start of my brand. My voice. My mission. Not a business plan. Not a launch strategy. Just a woman rebuilding her sense of belonging from the inside out and deciding that her story was worth being heard.

I didn't need a seat at someone else's table. I started building my own. That's what "Why Not You" became for me. It was no longer about asking for permission. It was about reclaiming space. Because here's what no one tells you when you're going through trauma: You don't just lose strength. You lose your place. In your friend groups. In your old routines. In the image you had of your future. But the truth I came to believe, and now teach every chance I get, is this: You still belong. Even here. Even now. Even if you don't recognize yourself yet. Belonging doesn't require everything to make sense. It doesn't require you to be the same as you were before. It just requires your willingness to say, This version of me is still worthy of love, purpose, joy, and space. And maybe that's the boldest thing we can do as women after loss, after diagnosis, after disconnection: to stop trying to "bounce back" and instead root ourselves in who we're becoming. I didn't belong to the fitness world anymore, not the way I did before. I didn't belong in the space of pretending I was okay. But I did belong to the women who were searching for truth, healing, and a way forward.

That's where I planted my new roots.
That's who I write for.
That's who I speak to when I say...

You belong in the story you're still writing.
You belong in the mirror, even when it shows a body that's healing.
You belong at the table, even if you had to build it yourself.

And you are not too late, too broken, or too different to rise.

You belong, because you're here.

Still becoming.

Still worthy.

Still enough.

On those days you question where you belong, a letter for you...

Dear you,

If you've ever felt like you were holding yourself together with invisible tape, this letter is for you. If you've ever smiled through pain, nodded through someone else's well-meaning words, or sat in a room full of people and still felt completely alone—this is for you too. I won't pretend to know your story. I won't assume your grief looks like mine or that your healing has followed the same timeline. But I know what it feels like to not recognize your reflection.

To question your place in the world after everything changes. And so, from one woman in the thick of becoming to another, let me say this with softness and sincerity: You belong. Even in the waiting. Even in the rebuilding. Even in the moments you're not sure who you are anymore. Belonging doesn't require perfection. It doesn't ask you to have all the answers. It doesn't mean you're never afraid or never tired or never lost.

It just means you're worthy, even when you're still finding your way. I've had to remind myself of that many times. Especially in the days when my body felt foreign. Especially in the moments when no one could fully understand what I was going through. And especially when the world kept moving, and I felt stuck between who I was and who I was becoming.

My story has cancer in it, yes. But that's not the only thing it holds. It's not the only kind of pain that teaches us how to begin again. This chapter isn't about the diagnosis. It's about the decision to keep showing up and to keep choosing myself, even when I felt like a stranger to my own life. And maybe that's what we all have in common. We've all had to reclaim ourselves at some point.

We've all had to look at the mess, the ache, the unfamiliar reflection, and say, "Even here, I matter. Even now, I belong." Your pain might not look like mine. But your becoming? That, I understand. Because it's not about the event that broke you. It's about the decision you made afterward, to stay open. To keep going. To speak. To soften. To love. That's what I see in you. Not your titles. Not your losses. Not the things you're still trying to figure out. I see your courage. I see your willingness to begin again. And that tells me everything I need to know about you. You're not behind. You're not late. You're not too different to matter. You are still worthy. Still powerful. Still home.

The next time the world makes you question your place, I hope you remember this: You don't have to explain your pain to belong. You don't have to earn your worth. You don't have to go back to who you were before. You just need to be here, with all of it. Breathing. Becoming. Belonging.

And if no one has said it lately:

I see you.

I honor your journey.

And I believe in the story you're still writing.

Erica Elliott

Founder of WarriorHeart Healing Hearts, LLC
Brain Code Strategist, Speaker, Counselor, Mental Health Advocate

https://www.linkedin.com/in/erica-elliott-ms-lpc-b90911150
https://www.facebook.com/warriorheartxo
https://www.instagram.com/warriorheartxo
https://msha.ke/warriorheartxo
https://linktr.ee/WarriorHeartxo

Erica Elliott holds a Master's Degree in Counseling Psychology and brings over 30 years of dedicated service to the field as a Licensed Counselor, Certified Brain Health Coach, and Certified Health Integrative Medicine Professional. With diverse expertise in various therapeutic modalities, Erica is specialized in Neurobiology, ADHD and Neurodiversity, Somatic Therapy, Energy Medicine, NLP, CBT, RET, EFT, TFT, Theology, EMDR, and the Gottman Method, all enriched by practices of Mindfulness and Meditation with an emphasis on spirituality. She is a mental health advocate heading a mission to equip individuals with brain health tools to master life. She is an Internationally Eleven Times Bestselling Author. As the founder of WarriorHeart Healing Hearts, Erica serves as a Brain Code Strategist, guiding individuals on a holistic healing journey that integrates mind, body, and spirit. Her mission is to empower clients to navigate challenges and uncover their true potential. By employing multiple healing modalities, she facilitates rapid rewiring for success, assisting clients in transforming their struggles into personal masterpieces. Throughout her career, Erica has had the privilege of guiding thousands on their paths to healing, viewing this work not merely as a profession but as a profound calling. With a deep passion for nurturing growth, resilience, and vitality, Erica is dedicated to helping individuals unlock the extraordinary life that divine intention holds for each individual. Having faced personal trials, she understands that healing flourishes in compassionate relationships. Together with clients, Erica cultivates the belief iron sharpens iron with strength and transformation, helping to forge legacies that inspire. For those seeking support or wishing to connect, Erica reminds us all: we are destined for greatness. Her motto is always- Be Blessed and Be a Blessing!Her newest book Internationally Bestselling book Breath of Heaven Manifesting God's Way is out now at all major outlets online https://www.amazon.com/dp/1968061371

You Belong Here: Healing, Friendship, and the Journey Back to Yourself

By Erica Elliott

I used to believe belonging was something you had to earn—by being good, looking right, dressing right, or being helpful and successful enough. But life has a way of showing you that belonging isn't something that can be earned. It's discovered. It's restored when you remember who you are and who God created you to be.

> *"For we are God's masterpiece, created in Christ Jesus to do good works, which God prepared in advance for us to do." —* ***Ephesians 2:10 (NIV)***

My journey began with the ache of not feeling wanted. Before I even took my first breath, there were questions about whether I should exist. At ten months old, I was living with grandparents who were not in a place of love but fighting their own battles, my grandfather with alcohol and my grandmother with resentment. I grew up trying to make sense of love that felt conditional.

Still, God whispered through the cracks. My great-grandmother was my first glimpse of unconditional love. She prayed with me and taught me to pray, sang hymns with me, and reminded me that I was seen. But when she moved away, the loneliness hit hard.

I remember being in second grade when my best friend believed something her sister said about me, and just like that, our friendship ended. Something inside me broke a little that day. It wasn't just the loss of a friend. It was the first time I learned that people can walk away even when you've done nothing wrong.

From then on, friendships felt confusing. I had friends in school and church, but even surrounded by people, I often felt like I was on the outside looking in. I would watch the girls who were popular, who always had someone by their side, and wonder, *What makes people like certain people?*

I didn't know it then, but that was the first analytical, psychological question forming in my young mind—the curiosity that would later shape my career as a counselor and brain health coach. I was studying human behavior before I even had the words for it.

When I lived in Chicago for a short time, I saw how some people could make friends easily while others stayed on the edges, waiting for an invitation to belong. I noticed how friendships shifted, how people changed, and how fragile those bonds could be.

Don't get me wrong. I had friends, even a few who felt like sisters. But there was always that quiet fear of being replaced and that it was about something being wrong with me. It seemed like with girls, there was always some competition, gossip, or misunderstanding. I was one of those souls who just wanted everyone to love each other and get along. Interestingly enough, I was often the girl others came to for advice, like they thought I had things figured out or something.

By high school, life became about moving out of that town and moving on with my life, not socializing. I worked five jobs my senior year while striving to stay on the honor roll, be on the business board of directors, playing in band, and preparing for both college, the military, and life. I didn't have time to hang out after the football games or parties. Though I went to a few, my responsibilities were too heavy. I knew the only person who was going to save me was me.

Some of those early friends are still in my life today, but our friendships have the kind of rhythm where you can go months or years without talking, then pick up right where you left off. That's a gift. But deep down, I always longed for deeper sisterhood—the kind of friendship where you could be fully yourself and feel safe, seen, and celebrated.

In my twenties, I prayed for close girlfriends—women who would feel like family. Soon after, God answered that prayer with Lisa, my best friend and sister of the heart. We laughed, prayed, dreamed, and cried together through so many seasons of life. But even our friendship had rocky times, especially as new people entered the picture, and moving also created some disadvantages.

Looking back, I can see that because I'd been abandoned so often, I was drawn to relationships that mirrored that pain. My first marriage repeated that same cycle—loving someone who kept leaving, emotionally, mentally, and physically. And I kept overgiving to keep the peace, to keep the relationship. That's what people-pleasing really is: self-abandonment disguised as love.

Through years of faith, therapy, and brain rewiring, I began to see that my nervous system had been programmed for inconsistency. I loved learning and teaching about attachment in the brain. Something that finally made sense. Chaos felt familiar. I had to retrain my brain to recognize peace as safety and put boundaries up for those who would use me.

When I began healing that pattern, my relationships transformed. I stopped chasing love that was unavailable and started creating space for love that was mutual. I began asking God for *healthy* friendships, not perfect ones, but real, kind, and growth-minded ones.

As I got clear about what healthy friendships looked like, I became healthier in them. I learned to cultivate what I already had and create space for new connections that matched the woman I was becoming.

The more I loved the person God created me to be, the more authentic friendships appeared. When I stopped hiding behind performance and perfectionism, the right people found me and I found the right people.

That's when I began attracting true, loving, life-giving friendships: women who saw me, celebrated me, and cheered me on. And when I healed my relationship with myself and with God, the man who is now my husband entered my life.

Healthy love flows from a healthy heart. It doesn't mean we never have challenges, but we work through them differently when the other person is for you and you for them. Mutual reciprocal relationships are beautiful, not perfect. It's not about what you wear, who you know, or being in the "right crowd." It's about *being the right person* and aligning with the right people who are walking in God's light alongside you. Beauty is in the Becoming!

"You are altogether beautiful, my darling; there is no flaw in you." — **Song of Solomon 4:7 (NIV)**

You can have beautiful friendships at any age. Healing doesn't make you perfect. It makes you clear. It helps you see who's for you, who's not, and who's meant to walk beside you for a season or a lifetime.

Here are a few steps that helped me build and sustain healthy, authentic friendships:

1. **Reflect on what you want in a friend.**
    Think about the people you admire. What kind of energy do they bring? Are they growth-minded, faith-filled, or compassionate? When you know what you want, you can start embodying that energy yourself.

2. **Be the kind of friend you seek.**
    Friendship begins with authenticity. Love the version of yourself God designed. Show up as her—not a mask, not a performance, not perfect, but your genuine, joyful self.

3. **Reach out with intention.**
    Schedule coffee with someone in your community, church, or local group. Don't wait for them to invite you. Create the connection.

4. **Vet with wisdom.**

    Just as you would guide your kids to date wisely, choose your friendships by character, integrity, and reciprocity. Is it mutual encouragement, or are you the only one pouring? "As iron sharpens iron, so one person sharpens another." — **Proverbs 27:17 (NIV)**

5. **Nurture what's real.**

    When you find a good friend, invest time, presence, and prayer. Celebrate each other's growth and give grace for the hard days.

6. **Stay open and flexible.**

    Some friendships are lifelong, others seasonal. Don't see endings as failures. See them as divine timing.

It doesn't take a crowd to feel loved. It takes a few good souls who make you feel safe, seen, and celebrated and create time for you.

Today, my circle is beautiful. It's filled with women who lift each other higher, a husband who supports my dreams, and a community that reminds me that belonging isn't something we earn. It's something we *remember*.

> *"For I am convinced that neither death nor life, neither*
> *angels nor demons, neither the present nor the future,*
> *nor any powers... will be able to separate us from the love*
> *of God that is in Christ Jesus our Lord."*
> *— **Romans 8:38–39 (NIV)***

If you've been searching for a place to belong, I'd love for you to join me.

I host several Facebook groups where women come together to heal, grow, and rediscover who they were created to be. We laugh, we learn, we pray, and we rise together. Come connect with a tribe of women walking the same path toward wholeness and purpose.

I also love helping people heal their *inner child.* That little version of you still deserves compassion, freedom, and joy. Inner child work is one of the most powerful ways to reconnect with your true self. It helps you release pain, rediscover wonder, and embrace the masterpiece that you already are.

"I praise you because I am fearfully and wonderfully made; your works are wonderful, I know that full well."
— Psalm 139:14 (NIV)

In my coaching and workshops, I use neuroscience-based, evidence-supported tools integrated with quantum physics to help people rewire their thoughts and energy and step into the upper-level *Quantum Queen* you were always created to be.

You don't have to walk this journey alone. Because the truth is: You already belong.

You can find deeper guidance, more steps to clearing blocks to blessings, and discover the hidden patterns that keep us stuck in various areas of life—mind, body, spirit, relationships, and finances—in my book ***"Breath of Heaven – Manifesting God's Way."*** In it, I combine neuroscience, scripture, and healing practices that have helped thousands move from fear to freedom, from stuck to soaring. You can find your copy at any online retailer like Barnes and Noble, Target, Walmart, or on Amazon at https://www.amazon.com/dp/1968061371

I pray this book has blessed you and that you use and share the tools you've learned. I have a book that expands on the areas of the brain and wiring systems that will be released by 2026 called ***"Brain Coding - We Repeat What We Don't Rewire – It's a Program."*** This book will walk you through the deeper science of your thought patterns, habits, emotional coding, and how to build a daily system to live in the fullness of God's design.

If you found this book helpful, may I ask you a favor to please leave a review on Amazon. Thank you!

As a Brain Code Strategist, I help people rewire with evidence-based tools and quantum physics to rapidly clear the mess and transform your life into the successful Masterpiece you were always created to be! People also love me speaking to their groups and organizations, teaching them tools in a fun, interactive way. I am excited to connect with you! Plus, find free resources on the link below. I am always adding new tools and teachings. Be Blessed and Be a Blessing!

Maureen Denise

CEO of Diva Designs Hair Studio

https://www.linkedin.com/in/dr-maureen-mcdonald-watkins-dpc-chw-cha-published-author-66b13559/
https://www.facebook.com/nesi.mcdonaldwatkins
https://www.instagram.com/nesiisflawless/

Maureen McDonald was born January 21, 1967, in South Carolina. With a lifetime of experience as a mother of two and a grandmother of three, a significant challenge in my early years demanded resilience, fueling my determination and discovering talents that would guide my future. My journey eventually led me to beauty and fashion, where my passion flourished. After graduating from beauty school with a focus on hair, I continued my education at the National Institute of Cosmetology, ultimately earning a doctorate in the field. For over 30 years, I owned and operated a salon, using my skills to serve and uplift my community. My love for bringing people together inspired me to host creative events, fostering connection and joy. Now, I hope to share the lessons and accomplishments I've gathered along the way, hoping my story may inspire and support others on their own paths.

Realizing I'm Enough

By Maureen Denise

Coming out of high school, life was supposed to be about figuring out who I wanted to become. For me, it was hair school—I wanted to be a cosmetologist, a barber. I was excited about building my future. But then, life shifted. I found out I was pregnant.

In that moment, I chose to put motherhood first. Still, I pushed myself to keep going. I went to school, studied, worked, and cared for my baby all at once. Two and a half years later, I graduated. But not long after, I became pregnant again. And that's when the questions started piling up inside me: How am I supposed to have a career and raise two kids? Am I really strong enough for this?

Somehow, with God's help, I kept moving. I told myself, I will be the best mom I can be. I worked, I provided, I made sure they never went without. But in giving everything to them, somewhere along the way...I lost myself.

I got into relationships that drained me. I gave to people—friends, family, partners—because my heart has always wanted to help. But the more I gave, the more I forgot about me. On the outside, I looked like I had it together: a mother holding down a career. On the inside, I was exhausted, unhappy, and quietly lost.

The hardest part was realizing how much I poured into others, only to not get the same energy back. That broke something in me. After my second divorce, I finally made myself stop. No new relationship, no distractions. Just me.

I remember nights when I'd come home from work, drop my things, and just lie on the floor staring at the ceiling. I'd ask myself questions I was afraid to answer: Why do I give so much to others and so little to myself? Where did I learn to ignore myself?

I don't have it all figured out. But I remember hearing someone say, "Sometimes when you spend all your energy on others, it's because you don't want to deal with yourself." That stuck with me. Maybe it started when I became a mom so young, and my focus instantly shifted to survival—making sure my kids were okay. Maybe it just became a habit I never broke.

All I know is, I'm still learning. Still working on choosing me. Because somewhere deep down, I know that in order to keep giving love, I have to remember to give some back to myself too.

One night, after finishing up in my salon, I finally sat down to catch my breath. The shop was quiet, and in that stillness, I heard God speak to me. His words were clear: "I need you to focus on you. I need you to declutter the people in your life."

I couldn't shake those words. That night, I went home and kept replaying them over and over in my mind. I knew exactly what He meant. There were people I was constantly giving to, people who pulled on me so much that I had nothing left for myself. So, I began the process of letting go—answering fewer calls, creating space, pulling back from those who drained me.

And as I did, I could feel God moving behind the scenes. Quietly, gently, He was shifting things. With the noise gone, I started to hear my own thoughts again. I began making plans for my career, and doors slowly started to open. For the first time in a long time, I realized that distractions had kept me from seeing my own worth.

Something inside me started to change. I began to feel lighter, freer. I wasn't just busy with my career anymore—I started being intentional about my personal life too. I went to the movies, out to dinner, even to concerts...all by myself. And to my surprise, it felt good. I remember sitting there one night thinking, Why was I ever afraid to focus on me?

To remind myself of who I really was, I made a list of my own characteristics. Writing them down, I saw myself in a new light: kind, loving, generous, full of heart. And I thought—if I can give all of that to everyone else, why not give it to myself?

So I did. And for the first time, I felt what it was like to truly pour back into me.

One of the most powerful things I began to notice was how God was lining people up in my path—people I had never met, never seen before. Out of nowhere, He started placing certain videos right in front of me. Sometimes it was just a few words in the title that caught my attention, but when I pressed play, it felt like those messages were meant just for me.

As I watched, I had a hard but necessary realization: I didn't have standards. I didn't have boundaries. That was one of the biggest reasons I kept ending up in situations that left me drained. I also realized I wasn't speaking up for myself. I assumed people should just know how I was feeling or what I needed. But the truth was, they didn't—and I never told them.

The more I listened, the more the blind spots in my life started to become clear. And little by little, something inside of me shifted. The old habit of always rushing to help everyone else began to fade. For the first time, I was truly enjoying what it felt like to focus on me.

Every day, I made it a practice: watching a video, reading my Bible, feeding myself with words that matched what I was going through. And the more I heard, the more I changed. The empty places inside me started to fill up with strength, with clarity, with peace.

Now, I'm not the same woman I was before. I've learned to speak up. I no longer let people take advantage of me. My boundaries are firm, my standards are clear, and for the first time in a long time—I know my worth.

For six years after my divorce, I spent time alone—learning, healing, and slowly discovering myself. When I finally allowed myself to step into a new relationship, I thought I was ready. But almost immediately, life tested me. Old patterns resurfaced, familiar feelings crept back in—the relationship felt one-sided, draining, much like the ones before.

This time, though, something was different. I recognized the signs. I realized I had a choice: stay silent and settle, or speak up for what I needed. For the first time, I chose me. I laid my thoughts on the table, unafraid of the outcome. If it meant the relationship ended, so be it—I wasn't willing to lose myself again.

When he couldn't meet me halfway, I walked away. And to my surprise, I didn't feel broken. Instead, I felt free. I had finally discovered my own worth. I realized I mattered. I enjoyed my own company, embraced my growth, and welcomed the wisdom that came with it.

No one is perfect, but we all have a responsibility to work on our issues—especially when they spill into someone else's life. For a long time, I was empty. But now I know, without question, that I am enough.

When you truly begin to love yourself, you realize something important—no one else knows your truth but you. And once you become secure in who you are, nothing and no one can take that away.

For much of my life, I didn't understand that. Somewhere in my childhood, someone made me feel like I would never be anything. And I carried that weight for years, constantly proving on the outside that I was somebody while ignoring the deeper work on the inside.

It wasn't until I chose to pause, to be still with myself, that I discovered the truth. Taking the time to really know who I am has been the greatest gift I could ever give myself. There are moments I wish I had found this space sooner, but I also know that every experience shaped me, and without them, I would not have received the fullness of this lesson. For that, I am grateful.

Clearing away the old lies and making peace with my past has brought me freedom. And today, I can finally say with certainty—I am enough. That truth is my peace, and that peace is my home.

Georgette Beck

Founder and CEO of Junk to Jewels Enterprises LLC

https://www.linkedin.com/in/georgette-beck-7a659387/
https://www.facebook.com/GeorgetteBeckWriter
https://www.instagram.com/georgette.beck/
https://www.georgettebeck.com/
https://www.bellahealinghearts.org/

Georgette Beck is an author, podcaster and entrepreneur. Georgette inspires, encourages, educates, and gives hope to others as they heal from the past, in the present, for the future while discovering and achieving their God given purpose. She is Founder and CEO of Junk to Jewels Enterprises LLC and Bella Healing Hearts Foundation, creator/host of Junk to Jewels Podcast with Georgette Beck, a speaker, and Realtor. Georgette's writing has been published in Launching Out, A Collection of Christian Inspirational Stories and Poems (Morris Publishing, 2011) and published her first book Junk to Jewels, a journey from brokenness & despair to beauty & delight (Fedd Books, 2024). She resides in Florida with her husband and two dogs. She is a wife, a mom, a stepmom, daughter, sister, and a Grammy to eight grandkids. Georgette and her husband can usually be found sitting by the Oceanside, anywhere in the world.

Whispers in the Silence: Learning I Was Chosen

By Georgette Beck

There's a kind of silence that doesn't mean peace.

It means absence.

It means not being chosen.

For most of my life, I lived with that kind of silence—the kind that settles into your bones before you even know what to call it. I was born into it. It was the air in my childhood home, the look in my mother's eyes, and the echo that followed me into every relationship. I never felt like I belonged. Not in my family. Not in my skin. Not even in my story.

I used to think this was just me—something broken inside that made me too loud, too emotional, and too invisible all at once. But over time, I began to see the truth: I wasn't the first woman in my family to feel this way. I had inherited the ache.

My mother was never loved by her mother. She was physically and emotionally abused, treated as a burden, never a blessing. Her mother—my grandmother—had survived the Great Depression, but she never learned to love herself, let alone a daughter. Pain had hardened her. And so my mother grew up unloved, and that absence became a legacy she passed down without even meaning to.

On my father's side, the silence ran even deeper. My grandparents were World War II survivors. My grandmother endured the Russian war camps and the long, frozen horror of the Trail of Tears. They immigrated from England to New York when my dad was a boy. He didn't know the language. He didn't feel safe at school. At home, no one touched or praised or saw him. One hug from his mother a year. His first hug from his father? On his wedding day.

This is the emotional DNA I was born with. Trauma, unspoken grief, and rejection buried under decades of silence. I grew up learning that love was something other people got. I was the tolerated one, the odd one out.

In my family, my younger sister was the favorite. Then, when my baby sister was born, I became the shadow of both. Unchosen again. I felt unseen, unwanted, and deeply ashamed of who I was. I thought there must be something wrong with me because why else would everyone look past me?

That belief followed me into adulthood. Into my first marriage, where once again I was not the chosen one. My husband was the golden child of his family—their pride. I tried to belong. I tried to be enough. But the rejection returned, and so did the silence. This time, I yelled to be heard. I begged to be seen. But nothing worked. My pleas became threats. My words—desperate for attention—only pushed him further away. Until one day, he left, and I was alone. Again.

And that's when I found myself on the floor of my closet, sobbing, asking God if He saw me. If I mattered. If I even existed.

That night in the closet, I sobbed so hard I could hardly breathe. My heart pounded like it wanted out of my chest. I begged God to take the pain away or at least make it make sense. I wasn't angry. I was empty. I wasn't asking for answers. I was asking if I mattered at all.

That was my turning point.
That's when God began to answer—not with thunder, not with miracles, but with presence. Gentle, steady, loving presence.

The first glimpse of hope came in the smallest way: a CD handed to me by my sister-in-law. *The Preacher's Wife* soundtrack. I put it on, thinking it would be a distraction. But instead, the lyrics broke me wide open. It felt like God was singing to me. Holding me. Rocking me like a child who'd waited decades to be noticed.

And slowly, He began to rebuild me.

We moved to Florida—my husband and I trying to give the marriage one last chance. It didn't work. The pain was too deep. The divide too wide. Eventually, he left again, and this time it was permanent. I became a single mom, walking through limbo, trying to keep things together while everything inside me was unraveling.

But even then—especially then—God showed up. He brought me to a church, a community, and a job I hadn't planned on but desperately needed. He surrounded my daughter and me with people who spoke life into my dry places. Women who didn't need me to perform or prove anything. They just loved me. Slowly, their love helped me start to believe that I might be worth something.

Still, the ache remained. Even as I healed, even as I stood back up, something deeper had to be faced.

And that's when God began revealing the root.

During a moment of prayer, God brought back a memory I had forgotten: I was almost 7 years old, visiting Poland with my mom, aunt, and grandmother. One morning, without telling me, my mom left with her cousins to go hiking in the mountains. She was gone for ten days. I didn't know where she was or why she left. All I knew was that she disappeared without saying goodbye.

For a child, that's not just confusing; it's soul-shattering.

It wasn't just that she left.
It was that she didn't think I needed to know.
That moment sealed a lie in my heart: You are not worth staying for.

As I prayed through that memory, I started to see the pattern more clearly.
My mom carried deep wounds, passed down from a mother who couldn't show love because she'd never known it herself. Still, I know my parents loved me the best way they knew how. Their love was real, even if it didn't always feel safe or whole. The emotional gaps weren't intentional. They were the residue of unhealed pain. My father, shaped by his own family's silence, didn't know how to protect or see me either.

The rejection wasn't about me—it was generational.

But the healing? That would start with me.

Little by little, God showed me who I was through His eyes.

He whispered to me during journaling.

He confirmed His love through books, music, sermons, and even chance conversations.

He gave me a new name: his precious sweet opal.

An opal isn't a flashy gemstone. It doesn't sparkle like diamonds. It doesn't shine with gold. But it has this quiet, mysterious beauty—colors hidden in layers, only revealed under the right light. That was me. And that was how God saw me: layered, rare, quietly radiant.

I began to speak truth over myself. I started to break agreement with the lies I had lived under my whole life:

- That I was unwanted
- That I was unworthy
- That I was invisible

Those lies lost their power when I started believing the truth: I belong to God. I always have.

Eventually, God brought someone new into my life—a man who saw me, pursued me with gentleness, and walked beside me with faith. We married and recently celebrated our 21st anniversary. Our beginning wasn't easy. Blending families brought its own heartbreak. His daughters were navigating their own losses and pain, and I often felt like an intruder in a story already in progress. Once again, I wasn't fully accepted and I felt it deeply.

Even now, I still hope for those heart-to-heart connections to bloom. But this time, I didn't fall apart.

This time, I could see the rejection for what it was—not a verdict on my worth, but a reflection of their wounds. I didn't need to force my way in. I belonged, even if others couldn't see it yet.

God held me steady.

He continued His gentle, relentless work of healing.

He surrounded me with women of faith who became spiritual mothers, sisters, and friends.

He taught me how to mother my daughter with a love I didn't always realize I'd received—but somehow, deep inside, had always known how to give. I loved her with my whole heart, even as I was still learning what it meant to be fully loved myself.

Looking back, I see that my journey wasn't about "finding belonging" in people or places. It was about remembering where I've always belonged—in the heart of a God who chose me before I ever had to prove a thing.

I still have days when the old ache stirs.

But now I know what to do with it.

I bring it to the One who never left me.

The One who was there in the silence.

The One who whispered over me, even then:

"You are mine. You belong."

To the woman reading this who's always felt like the outsider—like the one who wasn't picked, wasn't praised, wasn't protected—please hear me:

It wasn't your fault.

You are not unlovable.

You are not invisible.

You are not too much or not enough.

You are seen. You are chosen. You are loved beyond measure.

You belong.

You always have.

Leslie Fiorenzo

Founder and CEO of Business Speaking Solutions

https://linkedin.com/in/lesliefiorenzo
https://www.facebook.com/leslie.fiorenzo
https://www.instagram.com/lesliefiorenzo/
https://www.lesliefiorenzo.com

Leslie Fiorenzo is a business presentation coach, speaker, and best-selling author with more than 30 years of experience in leadership development, corporate training, and professional communication. She holds a master's degree in human resource development from Western Michigan University and has delivered workshops and coaching programs for organizations across multiple industries, including finance, healthcare, education, and technology. Leslie is Founder of Business Speaking Solutions and the creator of the 5 S.T.E.P.S. to Speaking Success™ framework, a practical system that equips professionals—especially those in technical and leadership roles—to communicate with confidence, clarity, and presence. She has spoken to hundreds of professionals nationwide and is recognized for her engaging, actionable content that helps individuals elevate their impact in meetings, presentations, and high-stakes conversations. Leslie combines certified coaching expertise with real-world business acumen to deliver measurable results for teams and organizations.

You Belong: My Entrepreneurial Journey, Third Time's a Charm

By Leslie Fiorenzo

Have you ever looked around and wondered…do I really belong here? In this job, in this life, in this version of myself? I've asked myself that question more than once, and each time, it has brought me back to entrepreneurship. This is the story of three attempts, each one shaped by doubt, resilience, and a deeper discovery of belonging. And with each attempt, I've learned that belonging isn't something you stumble upon; it's something you claim.

In December 2002, I found myself unexpectedly unemployed. At the time, it felt like the ground had been pulled out from under me—but also, in a strange way, like a door had opened. For the first time, I had to ask myself: *What if I built something of my own?*

I had overseen the launch of a new program and was the only employee certified to deliver the material. Although the numbers of our initial offering weren't what we'd hoped for, I was shocked when my boss told me I could either be placed on a performance improvement plan or quit. I chose the latter. Before leaving, I asked if I could take the program to market. To my surprise, the answer was yes.

What I remember most was the mix of fear and freedom—it felt like both a loss and an opening. Armed with determination, I jumped in. I said yes to every opportunity that came my way. If someone needed training, I said yes. If someone wanted coaching, I said yes. On the outside, it looked like I was hustling, making things happen. But on the inside, I was scattered. I wasn't building a business with intention—I was chasing money and hoping it would add up to something that felt like success. When I recount that period in my life, I often tell people I spent several years working a lot of part-time jobs trying to make one full-time income. And it never quite worked.

Looking back now, I see the real lesson in that season. Belonging in business doesn't come from being everything to everyone. It comes from clarity—knowing what you stand for, what you want to be known for, and where your true expertise lies. At the time, I didn't know that yet. But that first attempt planted the seed.

In 2012, I was recruited back to the very organization I'd left a decade earlier. With new leadership, I was able to do the work I was good at, yet I still felt something was missing. By 2020, that missing piece called me back again. I earned my coaching certification and felt ready to step fully into the work I loved. I was fortunate to have a mentor who encouraged me, someone who had already walked the path. And then—COVID. Practically overnight, everything shifted. When my mentor lost $100,000 in revenue in a single week, it was clear that we had to reevaluate. Several months later, a friend called and said, "You need to look at this job." I did and returned to company work out of necessity, but I carried with me an important truth: Outside circumstances may pause us, but they do not define our belonging.

I was working for a good company—but it simply wasn't a good fit for me. Plus, I could not shake the feeling that I was meant to be doing something different. This time, security wasn't my deciding factor. I chose entrepreneurship because I wanted freedom, flexibility, and impact. Unlike my first attempt, I wasn't chasing money. Unlike my second attempt, I wasn't at the mercy of circumstances. This time, I was choosing myself. The lesson: Sometimes belonging isn't about being pushed into change. It's about finally giving yourself permission.

Looking back over three attempts, what I've learned most is that entrepreneurship is less about strategy and more about mindset. Skills matter, yes. Persistence matters, absolutely. But underneath all of that is the simple truth that you must first see yourself as someone who belongs in the role of entrepreneur. Even when you don't have all the answers, you can trust that you'll find them.

For me, one of the biggest battles has always been with my own inner critic. That voice that whispers, *"You're not ready. You're not good enough. Who do you think you are? Why do you think you can do this?"* It's a voice that shows up at every stage of growth. But I've learned that I don't have to silence it; I just have to retrain it. I call this practice shifting from the inner critic to the inner champion. The inner champion speaks differently. She says, *"You've got this. You are capable. You belong in this room."* This is daily work. It does get easier, but the critic never completely disappears. The real work is choosing which voice we'll listen to.

One of the quotes I return to often is from Marianne Williamson in her book *A Return to Love*: *"It is our light, not our darkness, that most frightens us... Who are you not to be?"* That reminder helps me call forth my inner champion. Playing small doesn't serve anyone. When I allow myself to shine, I give others permission to do the same.

Another lesson has been the importance of community.

None of us are meant to walk this path alone. At times, community looked like mentors who believed in me before I believed in myself. At other times, it's been colleagues, networking groups, or simply reading stories of women who've gone before me. Each connection reminds me that I am not the only one learning, stumbling, and getting back up again. Belonging is often found in the simple reassurance that others have walked the path before you and you can too.

And then there are the small practices that make all the difference. One of the most powerful tools I use, and now teach my clients, is what I call *Prime Your Presence*. It's the practice of taking two to five minutes before any meeting, presentation, or networking event to get calm, centered, and focused. It sounds simple, but those few minutes can shift everything, turning anxiety into calm, self-doubt into readiness, and distraction into presence. It's a practice that reminds me, and those I work with, that presence is power.

What ties all these lessons together is persistence. Belonging isn't about getting it right the first time or never doubting yourself again. It's about showing up, again and again, even when it feels hard. Growth doesn't come from perfection. It comes from choosing, every day, to keep going.

Dear woman standing at a crossroads,

I see you. You may be uncertain about the future, unsure of what path to take, or questioning whether you're even qualified for the dreams tugging at your heart. I've been there more than once, starting over, wondering if I belonged, and wrestling with the voice that whispered I wasn't enough.

Here's what I want you to know: You are enough. Right now. Exactly as you are. You don't have to have it all figured out in order to take the next step. You don't need permission to begin again. Belonging isn't earned through achievement; it's something already woven into who you are.

When doubt creeps in, I've learned to ask myself two questions: *If not now, when? If not you, who?* Those words remind me that there is no perfect timing, only the courage to move forward with what I have today.

So, if you feel the pull toward a new chapter, trust that it's not an accident. Trust that your story is still unfolding in ways you can't yet see. Every stumble, every restart, every lesson has prepared you for this moment.

You belong in this journey, in this dream, in this life you are creating. And as you take your next step, remember you've always belonged.

With love,
Leslie

Looking back, what stands out most isn't the setbacks or even the successes. It's the quiet reminder that I belong right here, in this work, in this story I'm creating.

Belonging isn't something we earn after proving ourselves. It's something we choose to claim, even in moments of doubt. It's the decision to trust that our light matters, that our voice matters, and that the path ahead will meet us as we walk it.

So, if you find yourself wondering whether you're enough, whether you're ready, or whether you belong, the answer is yes. You belong. You always have.

Helen Kagan

Founder of Kagan Paradigm
Consultant, Designer, Artist, Author

https://www.linkedin.com/in/healer
https://www.facebook.com/helenkagan
https://www.instagram.com/helenkaganarts/
www.HelenKagan.art
www.HelenKagan.com
www.HelenKagan.net
www.WearableHealingArts.com

Helen Kagan Ph.D, a scientist, psychologist, healer, author, artist, pioneer creating art with intention to heal, is a creator of her unique HealingArts™ for 30 years. As a complex-PTSD survivor dedicated her life helping others, she synergistically integrates Expressive Arts, Fine Art & Art of Healing. "HealingArts" shown in multiple Galleries, Catalogs, Exhibitions, Countries, won multiple awards, named "Collectible Artist", is on Artsy.net and other platforms. A Bestselling Author with 5 books including co-authored with JackCanfield and JimBritt, works on 3 new books, has her column in 2 International Magazines. Dr. Kagan's awarded and published in PassionVista International as Woman-Leader(2023), Cover featured in

International Collectors' ArtGuide (2024), Cover featured as Inspiring Woman-Leader, IMPAAKT(2025), Top Leaders - Magnate View(2025), Holistic Wellness Pioneers - CIOGlobal (2025), and others. Helen believes in mind-body-spirit, in art being catalyst for healing individuals & society, and engaging Healthcare & Hospitality to encourage healing through art.

YOU BELONG. Reflections from the Journey Home

By Helen Kagan

Dear Reader. I hope my voice will touch your heart. I am honored to write for this anthology in the hope of deeply moving you with my words, experiences, honesty, and authenticity. To remind you that *you are not alone*, that healing takes time, that it's OK to not have it all figured out, and most importantly - to remind you that *you belong.*

This chapter was born from the quiet spaces between heartbreaks and healings. From the moments when I sat with my own silence and wondered if anyone else had ever felt this lost, this unseen, abused, neglected, unappreciated, uncertain about their place in the world...

What I learned—slowly yet stubbornly - is that *belonging* isn't something we earn by being perfect. It isn't found in other people's approval or in the roles we play to be accepted.

Belonging is remembering that we are already part of everything. It's the gentle truth that even in our messiest, most uncertain times - we are *not outside of love. We ARE love.*

A few years ago, I made one of my many "life-altering" decisions... I decided to be an author. Not just a writer, but a published author. Of course, I feared the responsibility of becoming one of the women to claim my Authority and reclaim my Wholeness. I am still not sure if *I belong*... as I am still in a process as a recovering perfectionist, a recovering abused woman, a recovering PTSD sufferer, and many other things I need to recover from to "come back Home" to myself. I am yet to be done with my process -from "Breakdown - to Breakthrough," as I am still on a Journey to un-cover my wholeness and re-claim myself.

But I made a choice. And I took the first step. Well, not exactly a very first one — I've probably made thousands of steps on my Journey of "reclaiming myself." I always wanted to feel "belonging" to something *bigger*, something *meaningful and important*, something that makes my own Mission-driven Purpose even more authentic, powerful, and on demand. Because I never felt belonging. I always felt like an alien even in my own country or family...

As all of us make decisions every day, I've made millions of decisions in my life— some great, some not, some meaningful, some stupid, some dangerous, and many of them were "life-altering." Being a scientist, psychologist, energy healer, spiritual counselor, musician, and artist - led me to become an author, probably because I had so much to say! to express myself in this genre as well. To feel *belonging* and to become one with the *Wonder-full Warrior Women* (WWW) community. This decision was not just random— it was brave and divinely timed. This is my time to share my HealingArts^{TM} and support my visions to help heal the world.

I felt I was ready to make this step on my Journey, to belong to a "WWW community," or to help create such a community of women like me— on a Journey to evolvement, empowerment, and enlightening; still in the process of healing, still in the rising, still in the unfolding of our Mission – Vision – Purpose. Your Journey is exactly what makes your *voice* heard. That powerful voice that opens doors to belonging to something bigger. And, as I keep discovering, you don't have to be done with your process to make a difference— your Journey *is the message*.

There comes a moment in every woman's life when the noise fades, and she's left face-to-face with herself— raw, uncertain, lost, and in search of a sense of belonging. My chapter was born from that sacred space. **You Belong** is a collection of 7 heartfelt reflections—part diary, part prayer, part invitation— written from the voice of a woman who has walked many roads, through many fears, many losses, abuse, immigration, traumas, tragedies, and many other things, to still be on a Journey to find her way back to the truth of being enough. To feel belonging. These reflections remind us that healing is not about perfection— it's about *remembering*. Remembering that we are not broken. That it is not too late. That we are not alone.

Each "Dear Self" reflection is a love letter to your own "becoming"— a voice of hope for the days when you forget your strength, your Truth, your belonging—to guide you when your heart forgets what it already knows: **You belong.**

Take these words slowly.

Take a deep breath between them.

Let them find you where you are.

7 Diary Reflections from Your Journey Home

1. Dear Self, You Belong — Even When You Feel Invisible

There were days you walked through the world like air—smiling so others wouldn't see the pain beneath your ribs. You tried to earn your place by being everything for everyone, hoping one day someone would look at you and *really* see you. But here's the truth: You have always belonged. Even in the quiet corners where no one clapped, even when your name was forgotten in the noise. Belonging begins in the soft whisper of your own Soul—the one that says, *I am here and now*. And that is enough. Place your hand over your heart. Feel that steady rhythm? That is belonging. You are not invisible to your own being. You were never lost. You were simply waiting for your own eyes to find you again.

2. Dear Self, You Belong — Even in the Mess

There are nights when your heart feels heavy with all the things you wish you'd done differently. When your healing looks more like unraveling than progress. But the mess is not your enemy. The tears, the doubt, the chaos—they're all part of the story. I used to hide the parts of me that trembled, and I felt so disconnected from the whole world. Now I see that the trembling is sacred—proof that I am still alive and kicking, still brave enough to feel, and even write about it. The truth is, we connect through the cracks, not through perfection. When I finally exposed my mess, I found people who exhaled and said, *"Me too."* That's when I knew - the mess is not a disqualification from love. It's an invitation to be real. It is sharing the Truth that is universal. You belong, even in your worst mess, because you're in the middle of becoming.

3. Dear Self, You Belong — Even as You Heal from What Hurt You

Healing is not a straight line; it's a spiral that circles back to old wounds until you can meet them with love and acceptance instead of fear. Some days, you can feel the past pressing against your chest, and you wonder if you've really moved on. But healing isn't about erasing the pain; it's about holding it gently until it loosens its grip. You are not what happened to you. You are what survived. You are what grew in the aftermath. The pain does not make you broken; it makes you deep. And yes, you are still allowed to laugh, to hope, to bloom - even with the scars. You belong in the middle of your mending. You belong in every breath that says, *I'm still here.*

4. Dear Self, You Belong — Even When You Don't Have It All Figured Out

There is no roadmap for your Journey to becoming. You don't have to rush, or prove, or perform your worth. I do know— you want to understand every step before you take it - to make sure you won't fall again. But life unfolds in questions, not answers. Let uncertainty be your teacher. Let curiosity lead you home. It's okay to stand in the fog for a while; clarity always comes when you are kind to yourself in the waiting. You are not behind. You are not failing. You are learning what it means to trust the mystery. You don't need to know the whole story to belong. You belong right where you are— mid-sentence, mid-healing, mid-becoming. And you are exactly where you need to be (according to Zen wisdom).

5. Dear Self, You Belong — Even After You've Been Hurt

Pain changes you, but it does not define you. I know the nights when silence feels like punishment—when your heart curls in on itself, afraid to open again. But pain, too, can be a doorway. Through it, you can learn tenderness, empathy, truth, grace, even love. You learn the language of survival. You learn that you can transform, re-build yourSelf, not into who you were before, but into someone wiser, gentler, more whole, and authentic. Every scar is a map of how far you've come. Every wound healed is proof of your resilience. You belong, not because you are untouched, but because you have lived, and tried, and survived. You belong in the quiet triumph of still being alive, still believing in love, even after your heart was broken, even if it happened many times. But it didn't break you. You are here and now.

6. Dear Self, You Belong — When You Choose Yourself

There comes a sacred moment when you stop waiting *to be chosen* and begin choosing yourself. It might feel strange at first, this fierce act of self-love. But choosing yourself is not arrogance; it's alignment. It's standing in your truth and saying, *I am worth the love I seek. I am worth the peace I seek.* You no longer need to shrink to be safe or apologize for being who you are. You were not made to fit into smallness. You were made to expand, to breathe, to bloom. Choosing yourself may scare those who preferred you silent - but it will save you. Each time you honor your heart, you come Home a little more. And in that homecoming, you'll remember: You've belonged to yourself all along.

7. Dear Self, You Belong — Right Here, Right Now

This is it - the sacred "here and now." Not the version of you that finally "arrives," but this one, living, breathing, wondering, trying. You don't need to earn your place in the world. You already have one. Feel the air move in and out of your lungs when you breathe—that's life saying, *You belong*. Belonging is not something you find; it's something you remember. You belong in your laughter and in your quiet. You belong in your dreams and in your doubts. You belong in this moment - messy, holy, authentic, unfolding. So breathe, my Dear. You made it here. And here is enough. Always has been. Always will be.

These 7 reflections are diary pages for all of us; who have walked through fear, abuse, trauma, doubt, tragedy, disconnection, and found our way back to wholeness. Our way Back Home.

They are not rules. They are just loving reminders.

P.S. For the Days When You Forget

When the world feels heavy, when your reflection feels unfamiliar or even scary or fills you with anxiety or panic, when you forget how far you've come—please return to these pages. Write these words and put them on our bathroom mirror. Or make it your screensaver. Be creative; just do it. These words are your own voice, whispering through time: ***You belong***.

You belong in the places you've left and ones you've yet to find. Your people. Your values.
You belong in your softness, boldness, authenticity, love, truth, your courage and strength.
You belong in the becoming— even when you can't yet see who you're becoming.

May these words be your gentle anchor, your permission to breathe, your reminder that no matter what you've lost or who has left— you still belong. Always, always, always.

I am truly grateful I decided to become an author a few years back. I was scared because I didn't feel good enough, and definitely not good enough to write, especially in a foreign language... But it was screaming my name, and I just had to do it. For people who need my wisdom, courage, experience, and honest sharing. For my unique HealingArts™. For our disabled HealthCare. For all communities. For becoming one of the WWW (Wonderful Warrior Women)! And of course, for mySelf. For my Mission, Vision, and Purpose to continue creating my unique HealingArts to serve people in need. And of course, to help heal the World.

Kimberly Tyler

https://www.linkedin.com/in/kimberly-tyler-a8849539/
https://www.facebook.com/profile.php?id=100094747320115
https://www.instagram.com/kimmijotyler/
www.brokenvesselholylight.com

Kimberly Tyler, M.Ed, is an international best-selling author with over 30 years in education and children's ministry leadership. A retired Education Director and dedicated teacher, she possesses a wealth of knowledge and experience in student success through positive learning environments and advocating for inclusive practices. Kimberly is an inspiring author with a profound gift for seeing others succeed despite any challenges that they may face. Residing in Northern California with her husband and extended family, she draws inspiration from the beautiful surroundings and close-knit community. Kimberly's writing reflects her genuine desire to uplift and empower readers as she shares stories that resonate with faith, hope, and resilience. Her unique blend of storytelling and encouragement has positively impacted the hearts of readers worldwide. An accomplished creative, her favorite mediums are fabric arts such as quilting and embroidery.

Restored A Message of Hope

By Kimberly Tyler

Life has a way of wearing us down, even when we do our best to stay positive and keep moving forward. You may have carried burdens no one else could see, quietly pressing on while the weight of delays, disappointments, and detours grew heavier. Perhaps it has felt like a long, dry season—your joy growing weary while others around you seemed to bloom. Behind the brave face, there may be a longing for more: more joy, more dreams fulfilled, more of the life you once imagined.

And yet, even here, hope is not lost. God specializes in restoration—refreshing tired hearts and breathing life into places that feel barren. Your story is not over; it may just be entering its most beautiful chapter yet. What looks empty can become a garden again. What feels dry can be watered by His living streams. Take courage: this is not the end, but the beginning of a fresh season, where God's restoring grace can bring forth joy and beauty in ways you never expected.

And maybe you haven't dared to hope for restoration, because hope has felt risky. But let this be a holy moment—a gentle turning of your heart back to belief. The kind of belief that says, *"God, if You're still writing my story, I'm willing to read the next chapter."* Because He *is* still writing it. And what's coming next is worth holding on for.

If that's you, then hear this clearly: **your story is not over.** The God of restoration is not finished with you. What looks ruined, God sees as a foundation. What feels lost, He's already reclaiming. This is not the end—this is the beginning of something new.

You are not forgotten in the waiting. You are not overlooked in the wilderness. And even when the world seems to move on without noticing your pain, heaven has not. God has seen every tear, every silent prayer, every exhausted breath. And He is not indifferent. He is near. Closer than the ache, stronger than the loss, and more faithful than the storm.

Your brokenness does not disqualify you. It invites the presence of a Redeemer who knows exactly how to rebuild what's been broken, cracked, and worn. Your life, right here, right now, is still full of holy potential because God specializes in rebuilding lives that feel broken. He doesn't just patch things up—He *renews, replenishes, and restores.* He's the kind of God who walks into ruins and starts planting seeds. He doesn't shy away from your mess. He steps into it with healing in His hands and peace in every breath.

The cities of your heart, once abandoned, are being rebuilt brick by brick. The vineyards are growing again. The joy that once seemed impossible is now growing quietly beneath the surface. You may not see the full harvest yet, but it's already underway. Restoration is rarely loud. It's often quiet, steady, slow—but sure. Like spring returning to a long winter. Like dawn chasing away the shadows of the night.

And friend, He doesn't just return what was taken—He **multiplies** it. He restores with increase. Not because we earn it, but because that's who He is. A generous, abundant God who rejoices in restoring His people.

He's not just interested in putting things back the way they were. He's after *more*. More joy. More peace. More of *Himself* poured into your life.

And it's not just about what happens around you—it's what happens inside. **He restores the soul.** The deep places. He brings a deep restoration that doesn't depend on external change. It's peace in the storm. It's laughter that comes from knowing you're loved. Its strength that rises when you thought you had nothing left to give.

He doesn't give leftovers. He gives *double*. For every tear, a double portion of joy. For every moment of silence, a fresh sound of singing.

For every lost year, a return so abundant you'll hardly recognize the life He's giving back to you.

You'll find yourself dancing again, not because everything is perfect, but because you've been made new on the inside. You'll look in the mirror and see a woman who has been through the fire, but has not been burned. A woman who walks in grace, clothed in dignity, with her head held high—not because of her strength, but because of the One who carried her through.

The beauty of restoration is that it transforms your pain into purpose. The same places where you once felt empty become the places where God's presence overflows. The same situations that left you breathless in sorrow become the stories that speak life to someone else's soul. You become a living testimony that nothing is too far gone for God to restore.

And if you've wandered, if you've questioned, if you've drifted far away—don't be afraid. He hasn't stopped loving you. In fact, He's been waiting for you with open arms and plans for restoration that reach far beyond what you've dared to dream. He's not here to shame you— He's here to embrace you. He's not pointing fingers—He's extending grace. He's not giving up on you—He's just getting started.

This is what He does. He restores. He rejoices in abundant healing and restoration. Not just a little. Not halfway. But fully. Completely. With joy. With celebration. With love that heals you from the inside out.

So go ahead. Let Him rebuild you. Let Him hold the broken pieces.

So come back to hope. Lean into the God who rebuilds. Let Him do what only He can do. Don't let the past define your future. Don't let fear tell you that this is as good as it gets. God's plans for you have no limits; you just have to believe and lean into them.

You are *loved* by a God who is actively restoring every dry place in your life. The joy you thought was gone? It's returning. The strength you thought you lost? It's rising up in an everlasting spring that bubbles over into a mighty brook that waters others. The dreams you buried? They're being revived and renewed again. Every area that has felt dried up, passed over, or too damaged to dream again—He is breathing on them with holy intention.

And most beautifully of all, *you're being restored, too.* Not just what you lost—but *who you are.* Your unique identity. Your individual calling. Your strong confidence. Your gracious smile. Your softness, full of lovingkindness. Your bold courage. Your unwavering faith. God is rewriting your story with grace in every chapter and beauty in every scar.

You're not standing in a graveyard—you're standing in a garden.

Something new is growing. And it's going to be beautiful. In fact, it's already begun. This isn't just survival—it's resurrection. This isn't just recovery—it's divine renewal. You were never meant to just exist through life. You were meant to *live abundantly.* And that abundant life doesn't begin when everything is perfect. It begins now. Right here. In the middle of the mess. In the quiet place of surrender. Take a deep breath. Lift your eyes, whisper a prayer, and believe that something good is happening.

Don't let delay deceive you into thinking God has said no. Remember, He's not just restoring what was lost—He's preparing you for what's next.

And this time, you're walking with wisdom. With history. With a deeper understanding of grace. You're not the same woman who first entered the wilderness. You're stronger now. Softer, too. You've learned to hold joy and sorrow in the same hands. You've learned that brokenness doesn't mean failure—it means there's space for the light to shine through.

You're not being restored to who you *once were.* You're being restored to who you were *always meant to be.* That woman is radiant. Whole. Anchored in God's truth. And fully alive in His love.

So say yes again. Yes to the next step. Yes to the healing. Yes to the unknown, knowing that God walks ahead of you. You don't need to have it all figured out—you just need to keep moving forward with your eyes on Him.

Let go of the weight you were never meant to carry. Leave fear at the door. Pick up peace. Wear joy like a crown. You are walking into a season not just of recovery, but of redemption.

And don't be surprised if your restoration brings healing to others as well. Your story will make someone else feel less alone. Your courage will light the path for another weary soul. Because when God restores you, it doesn't stop with you—it ripples outward. Your restoration becomes a testimony. Your testimony becomes a breakthrough.

Restoration is not a return to the way things were—it's a re-creation. A holy transformation. A renewal so profound that you'll wonder how you ever lived without this kind of joy, this kind of peace, this kind of clarity. You're not patching together old pieces—you're being made new.

And if the journey still feels long, know this: every step counts. Every moment of trust. Every time you choose hope over despair, faith over fear, grace over guilt. Heaven sees it all. Heaven celebrates it all.

God is not finished with you. The same hands that formed you, carried you, and kept you—are now restoring you. Let Him finish what He started.

Because you're not done. You're just getting started.

Jacqueline Goodwin

Healing in the Vessel International Ministries
Moving From Holes to Whole Coaching Business

https://www.linkedin.com/in/jacquelinegoodwin0507
https://www.facebook.com/lenisegoodwin
https://www.instagram.com/lenisegoodwin
https://www.healinginthevesselinternationalministries.com
https://www.facebook.com/BittertoBetterBook

Pastor Jacqueline Goodwin is an ordained pastor, prophetess, coach, author, and international speaker who has dedicated her life to helping others heal and walk in wholeness. As founder of Healing in the Vessel International Ministries and creator of the Moving from Holes to Whole Coaching Program, she empowers women to overcome bitterness, anger, and brokenness, guiding them toward freedom and restoration in Christ. A three-time master's degree graduate, including a Master of Arts in Practical Theology, Jacqueline brings both spiritual depth and professional expertise to her ministry and coaching. She is the author of Healing in the Vessel and From Bitter to Better, as well as a co-author of several anthologies. Through her testimony of miraculous healing, her passion for prayer, and her empowering teaching, Jacqueline inspires people worldwide to discover their God-given purpose and embrace transformation. Her life verse is Psalm 118:17 — "I shall not die, but live, and declare the works of the Lord."

You Belong: I Shall Live and Not Die

By Jacqueline Goodwin

Section 1 – Opening Letter

Dear Beloved Sister,

Before you turn another page, pause and breathe. You are not reading this by accident. Heaven has orchestrated this moment. Somewhere deep inside of you, a whisper has been reminding you that you belong—that your life still carries meaning, even when pain has tried to convince you otherwise.

I know the sting of betrayal. I know what it feels like to smile on the outside while secretly battling shame and bitterness on the inside. I know the fear of being labeled, judged, and misunderstood. And I also know this: God never leaves us in the hole. What feels like the end can become the beginning of a brand-new chapter of wholeness.

This chapter is my love letter to you. I will not just tell you about the wounds; I will tell you about the healing. I will not only share my brokenness; I will show you the wholeness that emerged. And most importantly, I want to guide you into the truth that you belong— fully, wholly, unapologetically—to God, to your purpose, and to the woman He created you to be.

With love and grace,
Jacqueline

Section 2 – The Wound

My story begins with pain that tried to end me before I ever took my first breath. When my mother first carried me in her womb, she thought she was simply sick. Out of desperation, she swallowed a whole bottle of turpentine. Later, her doctor was astonished to discover that not only was she pregnant, but the baby inside—me—had survived what should have killed me.

From conception, the enemy tried to destroy me. But God had already spoken:

> *"Before I formed thee in the belly I knew thee, and before thou camest forth out of the womb I sanctified thee, and I ordained thee a prophet unto the nations."*
> **– Jeremiah 1:5**

I survived the womb, but that was only the beginning.

At age thirty-five, my world shattered with three words from my doctor: "You have HIV."

Suddenly, the laughter that had filled my car on the way to the clinic vanished. Fear roared so loudly I could barely hear his voice. I thought, how could this happen? Who will ever want me again? What will people say?

Shame wrapped itself around me like a heavy cloak. Mirrors became enemies, reflecting not my beauty but my brokenness. I smiled for others, but inside, bitterness raged. I built walls to protect myself, not realizing those same walls were turning into a prison.

And sister, maybe your wound doesn't look like mine. Maybe yours is a divorce, a betrayal, or a loss. Pain wears different faces, but the weight feels the same. Crushing. Suffocating. Convincing you that you'll never recover.

That was my reality: a woman with a smile on her face and a storm in her soul.

Section 3 – The Encounter

But when bitterness was eating me alive and shame was silencing my voice, I remembered the lessons my mother taught me as a child:

When life breaks you, fast and pray.

God instructed me to go on a three-day fast. No phone calls. No visitors. Just Him. On my knees, I cried out like Hezekiah, turning my face to the wall: "Lord, I'm on death row awaiting execution. You are the only one who can pardon me. I want to live to see my children's children."

On the third day, God woke me up with two words written across my spirit: NEGATIVE and VICTORY.

When I returned to the doctor, he dismissed me as "in denial." But I declared, "No, I've been delivered." The blood tests confirmed it. What once was positive was now negative. What once was a death sentence became a declaration of life.

But God wasn't finished. He told me to go on a thirty-day fast—not for myself, but for the very man who infected me. It was the hardest assignment of my life. My flesh screamed, Why should I pray for him? But my spirit said, Because healing requires forgiveness.

On the thirtieth day, God told me to lay hands on him and call HIV out in the name of Jesus. As I prayed, his body grew hot. God revealed the heat was the disease leaving his body. That night, both of us were healed.

Jehovah Rophe—the Lord who heals—proved faithful.

God even gave me a revelation about AIDS: Appearing Impossible, Dying to Surrender. Healing required me to surrender everything— my bitterness, my anger, my control. And when I died to self, life sprang forth.

Section 4 – The Lesson

Looking back, I see that the wound was not meant to destroy me—it was meant to break me open so I could discover the woman God created me to be.

Through my healing, God gave me a framework I still live by: RAP—Recognize, Accept, Proceed.

- Recognize. I had to face my truth. Pretending to be strong delayed my breakthrough.
- Accept. Not accepting the wound as permanent, but accepting God's grace as sufficient.
- Proceed. Healing requires forward motion—stepping into forgiveness, faith, and a future built on Christ.

This is wholeness. Not perfection. Not forgetting the wound. But living free from its power to define you.

Section 5 – Closing Letter & Affirmations

My Dear Sister,

If you've made it this far, I want you to know how proud I am of you. It takes courage to read words that stir your soul. You are not weak because you've been wounded—you are powerful because you are still standing.

You belong in the family of God. You belong in joy. You belong in peace. You belong in love. And most of all, you belong to yourself again—not the broken version, not the bitter version, but the healed, beautiful woman God always intended you to be.

Wholeness is your portion. It was purchased at the cross. Walk boldly into it.

Here are words I want you to carry with you every day:

Daily Affirmations for Wholeness

1. I belong to God, and nothing can separate me from His love.
2. I am not defined by my wounds; I am refined by them.
3. I choose forgiveness, and forgiveness chooses me.
4. I release bitterness and embrace peace.

5. I am fearfully and wonderfully made, whole in body, mind, and spirit.

6. My past does not disqualify me; it prepares me.

7. I walk in freedom, joy, and love because I was created for it.

8. I am enough. I am worthy. I am whole.

Sister, declare with me:

"I shall not die, but live, and declare the works of the LORD." – Psalm 118:17

With unshakable love,
Jacqueline

Cynthia Armstrong

Founder of Release Recharge Reclaim

https://www.linkedin.com/in/cynthia-armstrong-rrr
https://www.facebook.com/CynthiaArmstrongRRR
https://www.instagram.com/releaserechargereclaim/
https://cynthiaarmstrong.com/
https://releaserechargereclaim.com/

Cynthia's heart led her to 15 years of teaching as an early childhood/special education teacher. After a head injury left her fighting her way back to herself, Cynthia used her education skills to learn a process that helped her injury. The amazing side effect was that the same process helped her resolve emotional pain and struggles harbored since childhood. Cynthia now teaches her Release Recharge Reclaim program to empower others to experience clarity, joy, and peace in living every day. She is deeply committed to supporting her clients. In her self care time, she loves Qi Gong, going to the movies, and traveling to new places. Her husband and two children love her quirky habits of inventing new words and mixing up lyrics in songs.

Rewriting the Rules: How One Classroom Lesson Helped Me Reclaim My Wholeness

By Cynthia Armstrong

At one point in my life, my children were already grown. I was teaching kindergarten, balancing the ups and downs of marriage after nearly divorcing my husband, and trying to carry myself as though everything were fine. From the outside, it probably looked like it was. But inside, I was restless, uneasy, and disconnected.

I was stuck, but not because I was idle—I was working, serving my family, going through life. I was stuck in the sense that I didn't feel fully *alive* in my own story. I wasn't being true to myself. I was doing what I was "supposed" to do, not what I truly wanted. Worse, I was so disconnected from myself that I couldn't even tell you what I wanted. It felt like I was a stranger and didn't belong in my own life.

And then, on an ordinary rainy school day, one little boy lit a spark that began to change everything.

"I Can't Run in the Hall"

The students had just been released from the gym and were coming into class. One of my most high-energy students came through the door with a huge grin and declared in a cheerful voice:

"I can't run in the hall!"

My brain stuttered. Something about his words hit me like a rock. "That's wrong," a voice inside me blurted. Not wrong as in breaking the rule—wrong as in the *belief* behind the words.

He was saying, "I *can't* run in the hall," which is very different from "I *choose* not to run in the hall." And that tiny difference changes everything. It teaches him, without him even realizing, that he is *incapable.* That his power is taken away by someone else's words.

And in a sudden gut reaction, I thought, *Don't let people tell you what you can't do.*

That one moment shifted something inside of me. I could see it so clearly: This is how it begins for children. This is how it began for me. We're told what we can't do or what we must do, and little by little we start believing it. The rules that are meant to guide become beliefs.

As the rest of the class was streaming in, I decided to make that moment the focus of our morning circle. I sat with my students and said, "Carl said he couldn't run in the hall. Is that true?"

A chorus of enthusiastic voices shouted back, "Yes!"

I tilted my head, pretending to puzzle it out. "I wonder what that means. If I can't run in the hall, does that mean my legs just stop working as soon as I walk into the hallway? And then they magically start again when I walk through the door?"

The kids giggled. "No! Of course not!"

"So...can we run in the hall?" I asked.

The room got quiet. I could see the wheels turning. Slowly, heads began to nod yes. "Yes, we *can* run in the hall," I said, "but why might we *choose* not to?"

That's when the conversation got interesting. Together we came up with reasons: safety, respect, avoiding chaos, and even avoiding consequences. The children also came up with a few situations when running in the hall might actually make sense, like certain emergencies or someone needing urgent care.

What struck me was how empowered they became when they understood the *why* behind the rule. They realized they had the ability to choose. Rules weren't chains; they were guidelines to help us work together and stay safe.

And that is when the lightbulb went off! It's not about blindly following rules; it's about knowing the rules, understanding the why of that rule, and then choosing!

The Rules Beneath My Life

That moment planted a seed that grew into some of the most profound self-discoveries of my life. I realized that so much of my unease came from blindly following rules that weren't serving me anymore.

As children, we don't get to consciously choose our rules. They come from parents, teachers, religion, society, culture. Some are helpful. Some are confusing. Some are downright harmful. And because they get planted in us before we're old enough to think critically about them, they become the foundation of how we see ourselves and the world.

I began to ask myself new questions whenever I felt triggered, stuck, or disconnected:

"What rules am I following? What are the purposes of those rules? Do they serve me?"

This wasn't about blaming my past or judging myself or others. It was about *awareness*. I did not intentionally choose rules as a child, but I can become aware and choose whether to keep or get rid of those rules now.

I remember explaining this to my husband one night: "Rules are like knives. When used correctly, they're incredibly useful. But used carelessly, they can cause harm." The same is true of the rules we live by. They can guide us toward growth and safety or they can limit us and cut us off from who we really are.

That was a turning point for me.

Written and Unwritten Rules

I dug deeper to better understand. Oxford Languages defines rules as: *"One of a set of explicit or understood regulations or principles governing conduct within a particular activity or sphere."*

That definition jumped out at me. Rules can be **explicit** (clear, written, stated outright) or **understood** (unspoken, assumed, or culturally implied).

Think about how many of those "understood" rules you're carrying that are unhelpful. Rules like "Good mothers always put their children first," "Nice women don't get angry," "It's selfish to want more," and "Your worth comes from what you do or how you look, not who you are."

Sound familiar? Those were the kinds of rules that made me feel like a stranger in my own life. They were sucking the joy and energy out of me, because they weren't aligned with the woman I wanted to become.

And once I started noticing them, I couldn't unsee them and I didn't want to.

Reclaiming Choice

Here's the truth I discovered: **rules are meant to guide us, not govern us.**

Their purpose isn't to strip us of agency but to help us live safely and harmoniously while pursuing meaningful goals. When we take them as absolutes, without questioning, they become prisons. But when we see them as guides, they become tools for growth.

I think this was part of what Dalai Lama XIV meant when he said, "Know the rules well, so you can break them effectively."

That shift—from being told "I can't" to contemplating "I choose"—is the heart of reclaiming wholeness.

So I began practicing it. Whenever I caught myself feeling powerless, I asked: **What rule am I following right now? What is the purpose of this rule? Does it serve *my* goals, values, and desires? If not, what new rule could I choose instead?**

Some unhelpful rules dissolved as soon as I noticed and named them. It took more time to figure out how I felt about other rules. This gave me the opportunity to dig deeper and become more self-aware of my true values and desires.

I found it super helpful to have conversations with trusted people—my husband, other family members, a coach—because sometimes my own mind worked hard to keep me blind to them. There was something about saying things out loud to others that helped me be more honest with myself.

The more I questioned, the freer I felt. Slowly, the disquiet gave way to connection. I began to recognize myself again. I came to know what I wanted and desired. And it was fine if those wants and desires changed as I changed.

This wasn't about perfection. It was about building awareness and practicing new choices. Over time, those choices created a life that felt true to me.

Wholeness Is a Choice

The little boy in my class thought he couldn't run in the hall. What he didn't realize—and what I learned alongside him—is that we always have a choice.

And so do you.

Reclaiming my wholeness wasn't about burning down every rule or rebelling against everything I was taught. It was about slowing down, asking "why," getting to consciously know myself, and aligning my choices with the woman I was choosing to become—not the woman the world told me to be.

It's about remembering that my life belongs to me, just as your life belongs to you...

So I'll leave you with the same question I now ask myself:

What rules are you following today that no longer serve you and what new choices are waiting to bring you home to yourself?

Priya Tandon

The Soul Sutras
Self-discovery to Personal Reinvention Transformational Coach
and Empowerment Mentor

www.facebook.com/thesoulsutras
https://www.instagram.com/priyatandon/

As a Self-Discovery to Personal Reinvention Transformational Coach and Empowerment Mentor, I guide individuals—especially women—through profound life transitions, helping them rediscover their authentic selves and step into their fullest potential. Through a holistic approach blending mindset shifts, emotional healing, and strategic goal-setting, I empower clients to break free from limiting beliefs, build confidence, and create fulfilling lives. Whether navigating heartbreak, divorce, career shifts, or personal growth, my coaching fosters resilience, self-love, and clarity. I integrate proven techniques in emotional intelligence, mindfulness, and individual empowerment to help clients align with their true purpose. My mission is to transform challenges into opportunities for growth, providing the tools and support needed for lasting change. By bridging self-discovery with actionable reinvention strategies, I help individuals heal and thrive, creating a life of confidence, fulfillment, and empowerment. I am also a writer and editor, publishing articles in Coaching Perspectives, Elephant Journal, and Medium.

Ten Seconds of Death:
How Ten Seconds of Death Gave Me Life

By Priya Tandon

I am sitting outside in my backyard with Buddy, my golden retriever, at my feet. A summer day at its best with a clear blue sky, birds on the trees, bees on the pollinators that I had planted, squirrels trying to outrun each other in their quest for food, and the constant humming of the air conditioner. I begin to type the words that are in me, aching to come out. These words are perhaps just a window to a house of relationship that was fragile, emotionally debilitating, and physically exhausting, with verbal words and physical actions that minimized my being. However, when I turned the narrative around, the story gave me the power to reclaim my being and made me whole, allowing me to begin a new life. This story is not of a near-death experience from which I came back. I shudder to think what that must be. Still, it is an account of death in breathing, death while alive.

Moment by moment, life comes alive in our body, mind, and emotions. Some moments are fleeting, and some we hold on to in our memory box. When we open the memory box and play its tunes, it becomes our past. When we participate in creating a moment, it becomes our 'now,' and when we start decorating and building a box for our moments to come, it becomes the future.

Call it life. And then death does its number, and we don't know if ever those moments existed or were imaginary in our minds. Sure, they must have somewhere as pearls of life. It is a thought to pacify me more than others.

Ten seconds are the frozen seconds etched in my being forever for deep pain, sorrow, anguish, and then a firm resolve—all in ten seconds was the death of the person who I was. I share a vulnerable piece of my life in a few words, without any embarrassment, shame, or guilt, because being vulnerable is a strength, right? And hopefully, somewhere, someone will benefit from this story.

The story goes back to the late nineties, when I was very young — naive, even—when I fell in love, and boy, did I fall in love! I loved this man with an open heart and deep love that went beyond any vows or promises. My love was not a fairytale love of finding a prince. It was a one-of-a-kind love that did not see that there was a dire need for support for education financially, was insecure emotionally, and had no guarantee that we would have a solid financial future anytime soon—the kind of signs that one would avoid even getting into a relationship with, yet hope for a happy ending. I only saw the person, not the imperfections, the lack of money, or the insecurities about the future. When he said he wanted to marry me, I hesitated, then committed my soul to him.

Fast forward, we made it. From fourteen-hour shifts, sleeping on the floor, and hourly jobs at restaurants and the front desk to successful corporate careers—an American dream with a white picket fence in Silicon Valley. I was proud of his accomplishments and of myself. I was true to my commitment and stood by him in the darkest hours, which were, by the way, more than the good ones. I had a hand in creating a destiny with my blood and sweat, which started with a zero. Sounds great, doesn't it? Except everything ended in ten seconds.

I had assumed the role of a 'rescuer,' being the 'stronger' one who had a solution to every problem we faced. I was left behind in my desire to progress in my career, ambitions, and even well-being. I became the giver who sacrificed to fulfill expectations. Now excluded from the joint success as a couple, unappreciated, and overworked, I was alone as a mother to a child on the autism spectrum. As I write this, I may not be proud of what I did for myself, but I had made a commitment to love, and there was nothing bigger to me than that resolve.

Diagnosed with depression and acute anemia, I filed for divorce. This was the death of a label to a relationship: Love carried on in my heart. I moved out of the home.

One day, sitting in the living room, back on the floor of an apartment as my temporary residence until the divorce gets finalized, I receive a text. I had an inkling before filing for the divorce, but now there it was. The ten seconds that brought me pain, misery, and anguish, and defined my life. The text had pictures of him and another woman holding hands, attending yoga classes, sipping wine, attending a hot air balloon festival, and dancing at a concert. I wanted to end my life. That was it. I wanted to die.

Death seemed more endearing than life.

I wanted to end all ...that is, until I looked up to see the angelic faces of my children. One is playing with a toy vacuum cleaner, and the other is making sounds of "vroom vroom" with his red Lightning McQueen car. My elder one looked up at my tears, dropped his toy car, and put his arms around my neck.

Why should I die? This question was the death of me and also the birth of me. After all, I had not 'bought' him because I had a hand in his success, and life is bigger than any betrayal or heartbreak. Those pictures led to the death of any remaining doubt, emotions, or love I had for him. Suddenly, it was calm, as if a weight was lifted off me. Maybe I was waiting for something like this to get out of the commitment I had made twenty years ago.

I shiver to think what would have happened if I had taken the thought to end my life into action. The two innocent faces unknowingly saved me. The arms of my elder son uplifted me and continue to do so even today.

You see, people will do everything in their power to let you down if you let them! I let the belief in love and personal responsibility for a commitment blind me. A relationship based on economics is not love; a relationship that needs negotiations and deals with conditions is not love either. Love does not betray, hurt, or ask for sacrifices. Is my belief in love shaken? Hell, yes. Will I believe in love again? Maybe or maybe not? Am I scared to be hurt? Perhaps!

But am I at peace with the death of a twenty-year relationship? Absolutely fucking yes! Why? Because everyone has to take responsibility and be accountable for their life, well-being, health, and happiness. I am creating my life, finding myself not in cubicles and corporate jobs but in the lap of nature, art, poetry, travels, writings, spirituality, community, purpose-driven work, and the laughter of my children. Sure, days are hard, but I own the days and nights now and am not ready to give up for anyone or anything in this world.

Everyone's path is different, and that is okay. Start by knowing who you are and charting your path. Maybe you want to rest your head under the shade of the tree along the river, live atop a mountain, and call it a life. Or perhaps you want to be an executive. Do what empowers you and puts a smile on your face. Living a life built for and on others' expectations is a fake life, and you are playing a character who will one day rebel.

Be authentic to yourself. The sooner we know, the better. And if you do love someone, then show up every day for that person, not in the way you want them to be but in the way you would like to be loved.

The ten seconds remain the biggest realization and most rewarding from the pain that I had to endure. It was truly the death and birth of me together, which I celebrate to mark my present.

Susan Tatem

Founder and CEO of Bright Path 4 Autism
Speaker, TV Host, YouTuber, LPTA, CGIP, Author

www.linkedin.com/in/susan-tatem-brightpath
www.facebook/SusanMTatem
https://www.instagram.com/SusanMTatem
www.brightpath4autism.org
https://www.youtube.com/@PuzzledParentsUnlocked

Susan Tatem, founder and CEO of Bright Path 4 Autism, is an autism advocate, coach, speaker, author, TV host, and YouTuber. Drawing on 30 years in healthcare and her lived experience raising her daughter with autism as a single mom, she helps parents of children with autism transform from overwhelm, fear, and isolation to clarity, confidence, and support. Susan teaches IEP strategy, services navigation, and life-skills planning that foster independence: job readiness, daily living, safety, and community participation. She shares practical guidance in Autism Parenting Magazine, books, on stages, and on her TV show Puzzled Parents (FENIX TV) and YouTube channel, @PuzzledParentsUnlocked. By spotlighting real issues and workable solutions, Susan equips families, caregivers, professionals, employers, and legislators to build stronger paths for adults with autism. Her mission is simple: Educate, Empower, Elevate. Why? Because Every Piece Matters

Dear Diary

By Susan Tatem

I used to ask myself in the quiet places, the children's hospital corridor after another appointment, the school parking lot after another meeting, the edge of my bed when the house finally exhaled: *Do I belong here? In this life? In this body? In this story?*

The answers came as letters I began to write to the uncertain parts of me. What follows are some of those letters, love notes to the girl I was, the woman I became, and the women I have met along the way. If you recognize yourself in any line, it's because this is your story, too.

Dear 22-year-old me, holding a baby and an armful of questions,

You don't know the words yet: IEP, autism, support services, developmental delay, guardianship vs. POA, but you will learn them by heart. There will be a day when a stranger (who will become a dear friend) says "Asperger's," a strange word you've never heard, and every plan you ever had for your baby girl will dissipate. You will swallow hard. Your curiosity will be piqued, and your journey begins.

Here is what I wish you could know now: Autism is not a verdict. It's a doorway. You already have what you need. You're smart, resourceful, calm in a crisis, stubborn, and love so deeply that you fiercely protect those you love. You will advocate until it becomes a second language. You will find people who see your daughter the way you do, not as a problem to fix but as a person with brilliance of her own. You will be exhausted. You will also be brave. The two can live together.

Own every room you step into on behalf of your child. You are the expert on her. You'll speak with authority. Eventually, they will listen.

Dear Body,

I owe you an apology. I treated you like a machine for years, one more thing to manage while I managed everything else. You asked for rest and I bargained with you: *After this appointment. After this deadline. After this crisis.*

Chronic pain has been the teacher I never would have chosen. It slowed me when I wanted to sprint. It forced me to sit when I needed to move. But I am listening now. I see the quiet ways you fight for me, how you keep a steady beat under stress, how you move me toward my daughter when she needs me, and how you stand me up to speak when fear wants me silent.

You belong because you're mine. You have taught me that asking for help isn't a weakness. It takes courage.

Dear Single Mom,

It's 2:17 a.m. You're sitting in the glow of the refrigerator light, eating a string cheese like it's a sacrament. The laundry is humming. The world is asleep except for you and the worry. You're doing the math again: appointments, mileage, hours at work, hours of sleep you didn't get, dollars you're not sure will be there when the next bill is due. You pick up the pen to write a list because lists make the big feel smaller. You are building something you cannot yet measure: a future where your child has more independence and choices because you never gave up.

Here's what I want to tell you: Stop. Breathe. Feel the mercy of God. Say a short prayer. "Help." That's enough. One day you will look back and thank God for the lessons learned.

Dear Daughter,

There is a story people like to tell about belonging. It sounds like this: *If you learn the rules of the room, you can come inside. If you can't, the room isn't for you.* We are going to write another story together.

Together, we will build rooms that fit you. We will make a plan for your adulthood, not because the world expects us to, but because you deserve a life with choices, work that lights you up, routines that make sense, and friendships that feel safe. We will practice self-advocacy because someday, I'll be gone.

Dear Advocate,

I miss you. Grief can be a calling card. Here's the truth I learned in your absence: Sometimes the baton is placed in your hand when you're not looking for it. I thought I was honoring you by remembering you. But I honor you more by becoming for others what you were for me. When I talk with a parent who's struggling, I hear your voice in the questions I ask. When I help a young person with a resume or a bus route, I feel your smile. You are still such a huge part of our lives. When times get tough, I ask myself, "What would you tell me?" Rest in peace knowing your voice lives on throughout my life and my mission to help others.

Dear Faith,

You taught me that love isn't always pretty; it's loyal. It sits in the room when the answers aren't clear yet. It holds the tension of *not yet* without withdrawing its hand. Your voice didn't boom. It nudged. "One step," you said. "One more." And every single time, there was enough light for the next square of the path. You promised to never leave me or forsake me. You never have. You promised you'd meet all my needs. You always do.

Thank you for holding me when I had no shoulder to lean on. Thank you for lifting me up when I was down. Thank you for the journey past, present, and future. Where you are is where I belong.

Thank you for blessing me with my daughter and teaching me all the lessons I've learned because of her.

1. **Wholeness is not a finish line.** It's the practice of gathering every piece—fear and courage, grief and grit—and blessing them into one life.
2. **Ask for help early.** Doing it alone is not proof of strength; it's a recipe for exhaustion.
3. **Celebrate practicality.** A printed schedule, a laminated checklist, a role-play in the living room...these are small miracles. No matter how small, take the "Win."
4. **Rest is not a reward.** It's a requirement. Sleep is part of the plan.
5. **Joy belongs in hard seasons.** Laughing doesn't betray your child's struggle; it strengthens you for it.

Dear Calling That Chose Me,

For nearly thirty years I worked in healthcare, learning the miracle and limits of a body. I never planned to be a coach or an advocate or a woman on a stage with a microphone. But life's funny that way. It grows in the cracks. It taps your shoulder after a thousand repetitions, phone calls made, forms translated, and skills taught at the kitchen counter: budgeting, laundry, bus schedules, interviews, safety, kindness, and sarcasm. One day you look up and realize you're crushing it.

I named it Bright Path 4 Autism because that's what it felt like when the fog cleared: not a highway, just a trail. I've watched families go from *What happens after high school?* to *Here is the plan!*

My mission isn't over yet. Someday, I'll watch employers learn to look for reliability and focus rather than misjudge. I'll watch communities thrive by making room and accepting everyone.

Belonging, I've learned, isn't a couch where a few chosen people lounge while the rest look on. It's a deep belief inside yourself. Create the rooms you belong in. Surround yourself with the people you admire and love. Life is too short to wish and wait. The only person standing in your way is **YOU**. The only one who can fix that is **YOU**. If you want things to change, **YOU** have to change something. Take action. Make it happen.

Dear Reader,

Maybe your story is nothing like mine. Maybe it overlaps in all the ways that matter. Maybe your question today is not about a child, but a career, a relationship, a diagnosis, a body that won't cooperate, a dream that feels back-burnered, or a faith that has lost its words. The details can be different but the lesson is the same.

You belong when you're learning. You belong when you're lost. You belong when you change your mind. You belong when the room misunderstands you. You belong before you prove anything and after you drop the ball. You belong in celebration and in silence. You belong when the plan is clear and when all you have is the next step.

If there's a ribbon that ties all these letters together, it's simple: Every piece matters. Not just the pretty ones. Not just the parts you enjoy posting about. The hard-won wisdom, the quiet endurance, the steady hands, and the questions you keep asking even when the answers come slow, all of it adds up to a wholeness that is not theoretical. It is lived.

Read this last line out loud, not because you need to convince anyone, but because you deserve to hear it:

I belong. I always have.

Sara-Ann Rosen

Founder of Settling Up in Love Coaching, LLC

https://www.linkedin.com/in/sara-ann-rosen-j-d-m-a-in-counseling-b800669/
https://www.facebook.com/saraann.rosen
https://www.instagram.com/settlingupinlove_coaching_/
https://settling-up.com/
https://www.tiktok.com/@settlingupinlove_coach_

Sara-Ann Rosen grew up in a multicultural family in New York City. A former attorney and therapist turned dating and relationship coach, she founded Settling Up in Love Coaching in 2024 to help audacious women stop settling and call in the courageous, aligned love they desire. Her Aligned Love System is an experiential, neuroscience-informed coaching process built on the four Rs: Reveal—make the invisible visible; Regulate—trust your body's compass; Rewire—shift the stories; Rebuild—design your future. Clients eliminate self-doubt to find the right person and stop settling for right now. An intersectional feminist and LGBTQIA+ ally committed to learning anti-racism, she centers empowerment, equity, and community in her work. She lives with focal aware seizures, and her writing explores connection, belonging, accessibility, and power.

When she's off the clock, she cooks bold, spicy, eclectic dishes, dotes on her tuxedo cat, and spends time outdoors. Sara-Ann lives in New York's Hudson Valley.

When the World Wobbles, I Steady Myself

By Sara-Ann Rosen

I carry a secret. Except when it carries me. It's a secret shaped by stigma. It's not what my body does; it's what people think it means. It can change how they see me and treat me. Some feel entitled to put me under their scrutiny. Some days it feels like a scarlet letter—*E* for epilepsy—pinned on me by other people's fear and disgust. I still feel small for a beat, then I steady myself.

Silence can keep me safe and isolate me at the same time. I'm still learning when quiet is care and when it's a cage.

My focal aware seizures started in college. The aura starts like a soft undertow. My mind lurches and skips backward, showing me puzzle pieces from my own past. I feel an urge to absorb them, to remember something important. Maybe catastrophic. That's what I make of the feeling in my gut—somewhere between nausea and dread. I brace for a full minute of divided consciousness.

The first time stopped me in my tracks on a bustling Tokyo street. It was my first grown-up trip to reunite with my first love. Did I just enter my own private twilight zone? No. I was still there. Standing in a river of bodies, I could still hear, see, respond, and move while one part of my mind surfed old memories and motion sickness.

The sequence is always the same. The images are games, in age order: Candy Land, Chutes and Ladders, Mastermind, then The Game of Life. I'm three, five, seven, then ten. Comfort-colored, with a chill I can't name. The path is mapped, but the rulebook won't open.

I've met the wobble at odd moments. On a train, on the phone, cooking, daydreaming. My body gives the same quiet cues. I steady my hand on something solid. I soften my knees. I steady my breath. If sitting is kinder, I sit. I don't narrate. I don't apologize for the space I take to stay in myself.

For that minute I live in two layers. In the foreground I am unchanged—I can carry on moving and speaking. But in the background the old images swirl by until the undertow lets go. "You're okay," I tell my body without words. "You're with me." When it passes, I don't perform a rebound. I keep the gentler pace I chose.

My frenetic hometown, New York City, taught me that complaints like "I'm slammed," "I haven't had time to eat yet," and "I can get by on six hours of sleep" are badges of honor. Productivity is a love language. Convenience is the altar. Health is marketed as another commodity, something we're told to purchase and perform. Optimize, track, restrict, earn. If you're not thin and tireless, it's framed as a moral failing even as convenience food winks from every corner.

Ableism hums under it all: Bodies that need slower, steadier rhythms are treated like problems to fix or defects to hide. There's a dark history under this. The old "Ugly Laws" made it a crime for the most vulnerable to exist in public. That logic didn't vanish—it shapeshifted into appropriateness and efficiency.

Many spaces only offer fitting in as a consolation prize. Belonging is co-opted by the gatekeepers. In spaces built for white, cis/het, able-bodied ease, "appropriate" can mean "mask." If you match the template, you're read as neutral; if you don't, you're asked to blend until you blur. I used to pay for entry with pieces of myself—tone down, speed up, pass. It worked. But it almost broke me. The older I get, the clearer it is: fitting in is compliance; belonging is a relationship. It is co-created or it isn't real. Fitting in is blending to be allowed; belonging is being valued in an ongoing dialogue.

My "authentic" self isn't a solo project—it changes in conversation with the space. So I notice which ones expand me and which ones shrink me. I choose the ones that can hold my pace. I let the rest go, even when my old survival brain would like the gold star.

Learning not to match the pace we're praised for is also an unlearning. If I pretend self-care basics don't matter—enough sleep, regular meals and water, watching my stress, pacing myself—my body issues fast feedback. The work is to receive it as information, not punishment.

These aren't rules to make me "good." They're how I steady myself. I plan my days around the basics the way other people plan around meetings. Meals, movement, hydration, and sleep are kept like appointments. I keep evenings quieter than my city friends. I choose shade. I carry water. I let a "no" be a whole sentence.

I embrace the simple virtues (hygge!) embedded in daily life. Small novelties can feel as joyous and thrilling as that microgravity drop coasting down a country hill.

Some costs are quiet and constant. Only a few states will issue me a learner's permit. For years, I covered my tracks when I wobbled. I put in extra hours at work before and after. I earned top performance reviews. See? Nothing to worry about. Passing kept me safe in the moment. It also kept me alone.

Sometimes the stigma wears a white coat. At a routine dental visit, a practice I'd been to before suddenly insisted during the appointment that I was untreatable without a time-consuming, baseless medical clearance to fill a cavity. They mischaracterized my seizure type—despite documentation in my chart—and disputed scientifically established therapeutic effects of the local anesthetic for people with epilepsy.

Heat rose under my skin. My chest went tight. Before leaving, I quietly demanded copies of my file and the official policy (they never provided the latter), scheduled nothing, and followed up in writing, which they ignored. On the curb, I felt both relief and the old ache of being dehumanized. In my car I took notes—what happened, who said what—and saved it. Records don't argue. Then I went home and did the unglamorous work: research, emails, forms, asking for a supervisor. Belonging, here, looked like believing in myself and advocating for myself.

I learned to keep a paper trail because memory smears after stress. I keep simple logs—time, first cue, likely triggers, what I tried, what helped—because patterns help me help myself. Paper remembers when my nervous system can't. I started simple—date, time, first cue, who was there, what was said, what I tried, what helped. The first time a specialist asked, "When did it start? What changed that week?" I had only feelings. Now I can answer with facts and a body story.

Patterns help me help myself: sleep debt, heat, dehydration, stress, exertion. And records keep others honest: dates and exact words turn "opinion" into "document." I keep copies of forms and policies, even when I hope I'll never need them. It isn't a fight; it's a boundary. It lets me ask for care or a referral without debating my memory. It also lets me advocate for something bigger than me and walk away when a door won't open and try a door that does.

Now, when the world wobbles, I practice steadying myself in small ways. I recenter with a long bath. I reschedule without a speech. No apology for existing. If someone needs me to explain more than I have, I don't. Safety first, then maybe another try somewhere else. I used to treat aftercare like a loophole—something I earned if I performed well enough. I don't anymore. Care is not a prize. It's maintenance. It's how I stay a person in a body that sometimes interrupts.

Morning comes and I keep it quiet. I drink the water I set by the bed. I turn on a bright light. I check my little log—not to grade myself, but to plan the day. The walks sometimes get shorter and slower, in shade if I can find it. Breakfast, warm and wholesome, happens at a table. I stretch my calves against the counter. I try a quick body scan. "You're with me," I tell it without words. I wear softer clothes. I skip the news scroll. I answer only what can be answered without hurry.

I start with keeping small promises—more green tea, five minutes of strength training, an unhurried lunch—and let it count. Belonging is pacing. I don't make up for yesterday. I make room for today. I steady myself.

Some days I still feel the pull to pass. To sand my edges. To push through. Old scripts are stubborn. But I am not auditioning for this life. I already belong to it.

Tonight I'll wash the same mug. I'll switch on a soft light. I'll set water by the bed. If a wobble comes tomorrow, I'll do what I've learned to do: listen, tend, keep myself. My world will wobble again. And I will steady myself.

Annamaria Solana

The Red Heel BOSS
Brand Visionary and Confidence Coach

https://www.linkedin.com/in/theredheelboss/
https://www.facebook.com/annamariatheredheelboss
https://www.instagram.com/theredheelboss
https://www.theredheelboss.com/becometheonlyoption/
https://www.theredheelboss.com/obsessed/

Annamaria Solana is a writer, mentor, and voice for women who are ready to reclaim their wholeness. Born in Hungary and now based in New Zealand, she is a solo mother of two teen daughters whose personal journey has been one of breaking free from self-doubt, rebuilding after rejections, and learning to belong to herself first. Her passion lies in telling the raw, unfiltered truth — the kind that resonates with women who feel unseen, unheard, or unworthy. Through her words, she reminds women that healing is possible, that resilience is born from struggle, and that joy can be rediscovered even after loss. Annamaria is also the author of the NAKED! series, where she explores themes of self-love, identity, and empowerment. Known for her honesty and her ability to speak the unspoken, she writes to help women feel less alone and more at home within themselves.

A Love Story of Radical Belonging: Your Naked Soul

By Annamaria Solana

Disconnection: Rejection

I've been in denial for weeks. How do I come back from the rejection of my whole existence?

Not feeling loved? Maybe. But does it even matter?

What matters is the weight sitting on my chest every time I look in the mirror... or avoid it.

I still can't face my reflection. I haven't for decades. I'm not picking myself apart. I'm simply not ready to meet her. The woman staring back feels like a stranger, shaped by other people's perspectives. She looks distant. She feels unworthy. Insignificant.

I wonder where I belong. Do I need somebody to rely on? To be a daughter, a wife? Denied, no longer desired. A big part of my life was built on these roles. And now... over.

When I stand in front of the mirror, I ask the questions:
Who am I now? What is my purpose? What do I want from life?

And the questions that cut deep:
Am I going to die alone? Will there be no more family holidays? Who's going to drive the girls to town, fix the broken lightbulb? How can I do this on my own, be the taxi driver, the cook, the housemaid, the businesswoman, the emotional support, all at once? How can I make sure my daughters won't miss out?

The mirror doesn't answer. She stares back, tired and hollow, like someone who has lost her place in the world and her way home.

I see it now: I've been outsourcing my happiness. Denying my needs. Betraying myself. I feel lost.

Realization: The Flicker of Curiosity

I still can't face the mirror for long. But today, something stirs in my chest. A flicker of curiosity.

For the first time, I let myself ask the questions I never dared to: *What do I actually want? What would joy look like to me if I had no limits?*

Maybe it's the longing for affection, the warmth of being held and cherished.

Or the dream of laughter echoing freely in my home again, without tension.

The desire for stability, where my abilities aren't questioned over covering basics and beyond.

The fantasy of walking on a beach at sunrise in peace, free from worries.

The simple wish to wake up with gratitude and excitement.

The mirror still gives no answers. But I am breaking the silence. Searching. More determined.

Life doesn't pause for me to figure this out. The uniforms still need washing. Forms signed. Deadlines, appointments, laundry, calls in the car. Nights of exhaustion, holding my daughters through their storms.

The mirror watches it all.

But in quiet moments, memories slip in like a soft hand on my shoulder. Childhood gatherings. Weddings. Funerals. Proof I once belonged to something bigger. My best friend from high school— laughter until we cried, loyalty without conditions.

And most of all, my girls. Their arms tight around my neck. Their voices say, *"I love you, Mum."* Even when I feel like nothing, they see me as everything.

It's as though the universe speaks through them: *See? You matter. They need you.*

Dear me,
You are allowed to want.

My girls belong to me. I love them unconditionally. And to be my best for them, I must belong to myself.

"Never give your power to anyone over your happiness."
— **The Red Heel BO$$**

Return: The Fire Within

I need to return to myself. It is not a fairy tale. There is no rescue.

It is hard. It feels messy. Some days I cry until my chest aches.

The mirror still shows a woman who is hurt. Afraid of doing it all alone and failing. But today I notice a small flame in her eyes. Determination.

So I decide: I will show up. Every single day.

Some days aren't about big wins; they're just about getting through.

Another morning rush.
Another wave of emotion.
Another night of doubts and overwhelm.

But each day I get through, I trust myself more. Slowly, I begin to believe in my own abilities.

And then a shift: **Desire grows heavier than fear.**

I want joy more than I fear failing.

I want stability more than I fear loneliness.
I want to thrive more than I fear rejection.

I wonder what is possible when a woman decides to own her story. What would a strong Amazon do?

Visions flood my body, almost too big to hold:

A safe, balanced, loving home.
Not one, but two thriving businesses.
Holidays with my daughters. Sitting across from them at restaurants. Saying yes to gourmet meals. Saying yes to life.
Evenings filled with laughter, inside jokes, and memories outshining wounds.

The reflection feels different now. She's no longer the rejected version of me. She is becoming the seeker. The fighter. The woman who refuses to stay down.

For the first time, I feel less alone. I sense the universe ready to meet me, now that I choose love, now that I choose myself.

Expression: Rising Stronger

I do the inner work daily. Self-discovery, self-mastery, self-love. I sit with things, I let go of what doesn't serve me, I am exploring. The mirror isn't so scary anymore.

The woman looking back at me isn't weighed down by other people's expectations. She feels lighter, freer. She is becoming whole, authentic, resilient.

It's still a roller coaster. Today I doubted myself. I cried. Then I called a friend who reminded me how far I've come. How much I've grown. He is right. I don't pause often enough to see it.

I'm grateful for friends from long ago (all the way to high school) and new ones who appear at the right time. *I'm not alone in this.*

I'm learning to trust my instincts. To respect my own boundaries. To honor my desires without apology.

And when I stay true to myself, something amazing happens. The world around me shifts too.

The right people show up. Not to fix me, not to complete me, but to celebrate me. Relationships built not on survival, but expansion.

I remind myself:
Belonging isn't in a role, a title, a location, or even a relationship. Belonging is within me. In my voice, in my courage. When I choose love and myself, everything seems to fall in place.

I was born fearless, limitless, curious. I know this. I see it in my girls, in old photos of myself before the world told me I need to be polite, quiet, obedient, and earn my acceptance. Before I was taught to ask for permission.

I saw the pattern in my mom and my grandmothers. Passing through generations of women, living life on autopilot. But not my girls! They know better.

When I look in the mirror now, I see someone who can stand tall, for herself and for her daughters.

Making the change won't heal the wounds but certainly will provide a better future.

Closing: United With Myself

I look in the mirror and I see her. The woman I've been searching for all along.

No shame. No guilt. No regrets. No doubts.

The old reflection isn't gone, but she is faded. She peeks in when I'm tired, when I'm worried. She reminds me there is always deeper healing to do. But she no longer rules me.

What matters is the woman standing here now. Fearless. Limitless. Rooted in worth. Not a stranger. Not a shadow. Me.

The mirror feels like a companion now. It reflects the truth: I belong to myself.

From that belonging comes peace. Freedom. Abundance. The ability to live fully, laugh deeply, dream without fear.

Dear Naked Soul,

You belong. Not because of anyone or anything.

You belong because you are whole. Because you are enough. Because you finally came home to yourself.

This is the love story no one can take away—the love of self. You are able to give, create, and rise from your heart.

Stand tall. Trust your worth. Live fully.

Because once you belong to yourself, you are unshakable.

With love,
Annamaria

Sherilyn Samuel

Founder and CEO of Pinky Promise Coaching
Coach

https://www.linkedin.com/in/sherilyn-samuel10b4a57a/
https://www.facebook.com/pinkypromisecoach
https://www.instagram.com/agelessallure40/
https://linktr.ee/pinkypromisecoaching

Sherilyn Samuel is an Antiguan born certified Life Coach, Social and Emotional Intelligence Coach, and Menopause Coach with a passion for empowering women to embrace growth, healing, and resilience. After a 34-year career in education, she founded Pinky Promise Coaching and later launched Ageless Allure, a branch of Pinky Promise dedicated to supporting women at midlife. Through her coaching, writing, and speaking, Sherilyn inspires women to take accountability, forgive themselves, and step boldly into the women they are meant to be. With warmth and wisdom, she equips her clients to understand and manage their emotions, build stronger relationships, and cultivate a life of purpose and fulfillment. Whether working with children, families, or women navigating the changes of midlife and menopause, Sherilyn's mission is clear: to guide others in becoming unshakable from within.

Choosing Myself:
Learning to Love with Boundaries

By Sherilyn Samuel

Dear Sister,

For as long as I can remember, I have been the one who listens, who understands, who forgives. Some people are natural-born storytellers; I was a natural-born caretaker. My gift was compassion, an instinct to listen deeply, to step into someone else's shoes, and to love them with patience even when they stumbled.

What I didn't realize then was that even the most beautiful gift needs balance. Without it, my compassion began to tip into self-neglect, leaving me caring for everyone else but myself. If someone hurt me, I explained away their actions. If someone disappointed me, I told myself they were doing the best they could. If someone leaned on me too heavily; I straightened my back and carried the weight.

And so, little by little, I disappeared.

You see, without even realizing it, my compassion began to look like giving until I was empty. Love became saying 'yes,' even when my whole soul was crying out 'no.' Belonging turned into keeping the peace, even when it shattered me inside.

It took me years and a broken marriage to realize that what I called "love" for others was often neglect for myself.

After my first marriage ended, I felt utterly depleted. I couldn't recognize the woman staring back at me in the mirror. She looked tired, hollow, and lost. Eventually, I sought the help of a therapist, and in one of my sessions, I was asked a question that cut through the fog: "When was the last time you cared for yourself with the same compassion you give to everyone else?" I had no answer!

That silence told me everything.

It was the beginning of my awakening: I am not responsible for everyone's well-being; I am responsible for loving and caring for me.

THE WEIGHT OF COMPASSION

Looking back, I see how my compassion became both a blessing and a burden.

I could forgive almost anything once I understood the reason behind someone's actions. If a friend lashed out, I would explain it away as a result of stress. If a family member neglected me, I would tell myself they had their own struggles. My compassion was real, but it was also one-sided.

Because here's the truth: When your heart bends only toward others, it leaves no room for yourself.

I can remember countless times when I said yes out of guilt, when I poured into people who never poured back, and when I worked tirelessly to make sure others were cared for, even if I was unraveling inside.

On the outside, it looked noble. On the inside, it was self-erasure.

My therapist helped me see that my constant giving wasn't only compassion; it was also self-abandonment. I had been pouring into others so much that I had left nothing for myself.

Some people are natural givers; we love deeply, support endlessly, and always find a way to show up. But those same people often struggle to receive. Rest feels guilty. Asking for help feels heavy. Being cared for feels uncomfortable. If that sounds familiar, pause and ask yourself: Where did I learn that my worth is tied only to what I give? The truth is, real connection is not one-sided; there must be balance. You are not only here to give love. You are worthy of receiving it too. That was the hard lesson: Love without balance is not real love. When it costs you your wholeness, it stops being love and becomes self-abandonment.

THE AWAKENING

The day I finally whispered to myself, "I deserve love too," was the day everything began to change.

It didn't happen overnight. Healing rarely does. At first, the idea felt almost selfish. I was so used to putting myself last that the thought of putting myself first felt wrong.

But slowly, I began to recondition my mind.

I started practicing affirmations in the mirror, even when I didn't believe them:

"I am worthy of compassion."

"It's okay to say no."

"My needs matter."

I journaled my feelings instead of swallowing them. I learned to pause before saying yes. I practiced setting small boundaries, even if it was as simple as saying, "I can't talk right now, but let's connect later."

I will never forget the first time I said a true, firm no to someone who expected me to bend. My voice trembled, my hands shook, and afterward, I cried. But underneath the fear and guilt was a surprising feeling of relief. I felt like I had just given myself permission to breathe. That is when I realized: Saying no to others is sometimes the deepest yes to myself.

LESSONS IN SAYING NO & LETTING GO

Through this journey, I discovered that love without boundaries is not love at all—it's depletion. I also learned that sometimes the most compassionate act we can do is to step back.

Here are the lessons I carry with me now:

When to Say "No"

When you are consistently hurt or exhausted.
If a relationship constantly drains you, leaves you confused, or requires you to shrink yourself just to feel worthy, it's time to protect your energy! I know this too well. For years, I tolerated exhaustion in the name of loyalty. Now, I understand that exhaustion is not love's proof; it is love's absence.

When you are responsible for someone else's needs.
Relationships are not meant to be a full-time job where only one person is on the clock. You are not responsible for fixing, saving, or carrying every soul you meet. That burden will crush you if you let it.

When a relationship hinders your growth.
Any connection that clips your wings is void of love and respect. Love should make you freer, not smaller. I would once stay in relationships that stunted my growth out of what I thought was loyalty. Today, I choose growth, even if it requires solitude.

When you are settling for "almost."
Almost chosen, almost respected, almost cared for—these are counterfeits of love. You deserve the real thing.

When to Let Go

When your boundaries are ignored.
If you clearly state your needs and they are continually disrespected, it's a sign: Letting go may be the only way to honor yourself.

When the relationship is one-sided.
Love requires mutual effort. If you are the only one fighting, holding, or showing up, then you are carrying a shadow, not a partner or a friend.

When you need to prioritize your peace.
Peace is not a luxury; it's essential. If a relationship costs your peace, it is too expensive.

When love means giving up your freedom.
True love does not control. Sometimes the kindest thing you can do for both of you is to release your grip, let them walk their path, and bless them on their way.

THE ONGOING JOURNEY

Choosing myself has not been a single moment but an ongoing practice.

Some days, I slip back into old habits, and I say 'yes' when I want to say no; I put someone else's comfort ahead of my own. When that happens, I remind myself: Healing is not linear. What matters is that I notice. That I pause. That I return to myself again and again.

Self-compassion is now the rhythm of my life. I allow myself to grieve, to rest, to fail, and to rise without setting a stopwatch on my healing. I surround myself with people who give as much as they take. I journal, I pray, and I breathe deeply into my own belonging.

I have learned that belonging does not come from how many people you hold together. Belonging begins inside, when you finally hold yourself.

CLOSING LETTER

So, dear one, if you are reading this with tears in your eyes because you have given until you are empty, let me whisper these truths into your heart:

You are not responsible for carrying everyone else's story.

You are not here only to fix, to please, and to forgive endlessly while forgetting yourself.

You are here to live fully. To laugh deeply. To rest without guilt. To love without erasing yourself.

Please remember saying no does not make you unkind; it makes you whole. Letting go does not mean you didn't love enough; it means you finally love yourself, too.

And if you have ever wondered, "Do I belong?" The answer is yes! You belong here, in your own story, in your own skin, in your own heart!

With love, always.
Sherilyn

Carrie Aboytes

Light the Way: Faith, Love & Music
Morning DJ

https://www.facebook.com/carrie.law.35
https://live365.com/station/Love-Leads-the-Way-a96984

Carrie is a mom with three grown boys, a beautiful daughter-in-law and a precious grandson. She is passionate about preserving the joy and the happiness we freely experience as children. Her heart's desire is to serve the people she encounters, to remind them that they are never alone, and share the love and light of the Father. She is always smiling and wants her faith to be alive – to dance, to sing and to love with everything that she is! Every day is a new opportunity to continue to grow and learn so that she can be a better Carrie tomorrow than she is today. She has daily conversations with the Father, counts her blessings constantly, tries to embrace every day with her whole heart, and believes with every fiber of her being in the power of a cha-cha! One of these days, she's gonna paint the whole world yellow!

You Belong Here

By Carrie Aboytes

Any month, this year... almost midnight...

It's too dark... And the darkness echoes... It echoes off the walls, through your ears, inside your head... And it doesn't stop...

It still feels like a dream...

I know it was hard. I know it was something that you never thought you'd ever be doing. Never thought it would take so much effort just to breathe...

He was gone. But so were they... How could they leave you when they still felt like they were attached to your heart... Your heart was always in sync with theirs since before they were born... But they were all gone... And you were alone.

You stood and yelled. You screamed it. You sobbed it... It was primal, brought forth from the bottom of your feet, ripping through your entire body...

Where do I fit?

Why can't I fit?

I just want to belong.

Why is this happening???

I did everything right. Or did I? Is it my fault? All the yelling. The heated arguments. Oh my god. It is my fault. Please. Oh please. I'm so sorry...

And your heart was tossed in a closet and all rational thought was hidden in a dusty old shoebox shoved underneath the bed.

But I heard you crying...

I heard the sobs that came from the bottom of your stomach. I could feel the gut-wrenching pain of all sorts of ugly things that you couldn't face finally burst forth from the overstuffed closet you have inside of you, the one where you kept shoving everything into for years.

And I saw the tears...

The tears that poured out of your eyes, your ears, your chest... in buckets... pulled from deep inside where the pain from being alone pooled... thick and sticky like a thick tar. Because the things you didn't talk about made you feel dirty, like an outsider. And so you saved them... You held them deep inside where you thought they'd stay forgotten...

He left. And then they left. And then you left. You got in the car and you drove to town to go get something to eat and you came back shredded... You didn't know what you even liked to eat.

They didn't love me enough? Why didn't they love me enough?

But how can you belong if you don't know who you are? You don't even know what you like to eat...

But I know.

I know who you are. And you know who you are. Because I am you.

I can see you. I can see me. I can see us.

It's not that they didn't love you—it's that you forgot to love you first. You forgot to love you when he was yelling at you... when he made you cry... when you wished that he would just hit you so that it would end faster... You forgot to love you when you felt guilty about your children hiding in the closet. You forgot to love you when your oldest son would take the physical abuse that you wished for yourself. You forgot to love you when you accepted the blame for being a bad wife... a bad mother... for being all the things he called you and knowing in your heart that he was right.... But he wasn't...

Where is your place? Do you even deserve one?

You have one. You're not lost. Trust me—I KNOW that you have a place.

You just forgot... You forgot that you belong to this world because the Father in heaven knew that the world needed you. And He loves you.

You're not just fluff. You're necessary.

Required.

Important.

You have a defined place in this world that is all yours. It has your name on it.

Take your hands away from your mouth and speak.

Open your eyes and see.

You are there, underneath all the layers of rotted, complicated, unnecessary trash that you just need to bag up and throw out...

See the amazing mind.

See the beautiful heart.

Feel the radiance and the warmth of your soul... the amazing soul that still carries the vital core of your essence... as it was always meant to be...

It holds the you that smiled and laughed as a child. The one that would skip happily in the sunshine and joyfully splash in the puddles when it rained. The one that would be happy with a yellow balloon tied around her wrist. The one who would wrap herself up in her bedsheets like a flamenco dancer and cha-cha like she was on a grand stage.

The Father who deemed you necessary is still within you, waking you up every morning, trying to get you to find the blessings in every moment. They are your moments. Your blessings. Claim them. Claim your place. Love yourself. And smile. Because YOU BELONG HERE.

Get rid of that stupid soundtrack that plays on in your mind—the one from your past that plays every time something triggers a memory of before... It's played so many times, you're not even sure anymore... Is it even his voice? Or is it yours?

It made you feel ugly and stupid... and just LESS...

You are NOT fucking worthless...

I know, when he left, your whole world changed... I know that it feels like you are holding onto the bumper of an old pickup, and it's just dragging you... your fingers cramping and your knees raking the dirt road it's barreling down... All you have to do is let go and it won't hurt anymore... I promise. I know that you're afraid to let go because it feels like you'll be left with nothing... And you've been holding on for so long... so long that it will be painful to let go... like a tight grip that gives way to that sharp pain when you finally find a way to uncurl your fingers. And wasn't he everything to you? You were everything when you were with him... weren't you? And now, what are you? And even though it wasn't a pretty picture, you were a piece of that whole puzzle... of that whole life...

Little did you realize... that when you let go, you won't be left with nothing. You'll be left with everything. That puzzle piece simply didn't belong there. It belonged to a different picture. You spent an inordinate amount of time trying to fit yourself into a space where you would never fit. You tried so hard but that space was never meant for you. The Father never meant for you to live in such pain.

And you panicked. You were terrified because even though it was awful, without it, you were lost. Because you thought that was your place. Because you thought that was your picture. Because, for the longest time, you KNEW that that was where you belonged. But you didn't.

Eventually, you had to let go of the bumper. You just couldn't hold on any longer. My love, you weren't supposed to. The Father never meant for you to hang on to something so ugly. And you picked yourself up and you went home. You couldn't see opportunities. You saw blank white pages, blank white walls... So much white... so much sterile, cold, empty, white...

So you painted your whole room yellow... even the ceiling... And the first time the sun came in, the light danced and the walls smiled. Because the light that came in was warm. And when it touched the face of the woman, the walls remembered her from before. They knew the girl in this yellow room. She could dance. And smile. And twirl. And sing.

The girl is there inside of you. She always was.

Be brave and let her out.

So that she can twirl and sing and dance.

So that joy can bubble out of her as she laughs.

So that her eyes can smile.

Talitha Koum, my daughter... arise, little girl—no more sleeping.

It's time to wake up and be who you were always meant to be.

Are you listening to me? I know that you can do it. I can feel it with all my heart.

Now put down the mirror and just do it.

Where do you belong? You belong here. In the yellow room. Where the light of the Spirit streams in with the sun. Such a beautiful warm light that dances on the walls. See the way the Spirit swirls and streams around you like glitter... And feel the light that surrounds you, the one that comes from your soul, with the joy that has been released at last...

This is your place. This is your time. Embrace it. You're awake now. YOU ARE HERE. I AM HERE. WE ARE HERE. Where we belong.

Time to claim your life. Time to remember who you are and be who you were always meant to be. Time to grow and blossom. Time to be happy. It's time to cha-cha...

JOIN THE MOVEMENT!
#BAUW

Becoming An Unstoppable Woman
With She Rises Studios

She Rises Studios was founded by Hanna Olivas and Adriana Luna Carlos, the mother-daughter duo, in mid-2020 as they saw a need to help empower women worldwide. They are the podcast hosts of the *She Rises Studios Podcast* and Amazon best-selling authors and motivational speakers who travel the world. Hanna and Adriana are the movement creators of #BAUW - Becoming An Unstoppable Woman: The movement has been created to universally impact women of all ages, at whatever stage of life, to overcome insecurities, and adversities, and develop an unstoppable mindset. She Rises Studios educates, celebrates, and empowers women globally.

Looking to Join Us in our Next Anthology or Publish YOUR Own?

She Rises Studios Publishing offers full-service publishing, marketing, book tour, and campaign services. For more information, contact info@sherisesstudios.com

We are always looking for women who want to share their stories and expertise and feature their businesses on our podcasts, in our books, and in our magazines.

SEE WHAT WE DO

OUR PODCAST

OUR BOOKS

OUR SERVICES

Be featured in the Becoming An Unstoppable Woman magazine, published in 13 countries and sold in all major retailers. Get the visibility you need to LEVEL UP in your business!

Have your own TV show streamed across major platforms like Roku TV, Amazon Fire Stick, Apple TV and more!

Learn to leverage your expertise. Build your online presence and grow your audience with FENIX TV.
https://fenixtv.sherisesstudios.com/

Visit www.SheRisesStudios.com to see how YOU can join the #BAUW movement and help your community to achieve the UNSTOPPABLE mindset.

Have you checked out the *She Rises Studios Podcast?*

Find us on all MAJOR platforms: Spotify, IHeartRadio, Apple Podcasts, Google Podcasts, etc.

Looking to become a sponsor or build a partnership?

Email us at info@sherisesstudios.com